Medical Match

Ann Gianola

Richmond READERS

LEVEL 1

(500 headwords)
Maria's Dilemma
Oscar
Jack's Game
The Boy from Yesterday
The Black Mountain

LEVEL 2

(800 headwords)
Jason Causes Chaos
Craigen Castle Mystery
The Road through the Hills and othes stories
Where's Mauriac?
Saturday Storm

LEVEL 3

(1200 headwords)
A Trip to the Stars
Dr Jekyll and Mr Hyde
The Canterville Ghost and Other Stories
Cold Feet
Frankenstein
P.R. and Prejudice

LEVEL 4

(1800 headwords)
A Trip to London
Dracula   Jane Eyre
The Adventures of Tom Sawyer
Sense and Sensibility
William and Kate: A Royal Romance
A Floral Arrangement

LEVEL 5

(2600+ headwords)
Steve Jobs: the man behind Apple
Elizabeth II: The Diamond Queen
Sherlock Holmes & the Oxford murders

Contents

Chapter 1: Gloria Navarro: RN 4

Chapter 2: Love Blossoms on the Bus 7

Chapter 3: An Embarrassing Lie 10

Chapter 4: A Friend Offended 13

Chapter 5: Antonio's Story 16

Chapter 6: A Day Off for Gloria 19

Chapter 7: A Disastrous Date 23

Chapter 8: A Life Saved 27

Chapter 9: Ketchup Required 31

Chapter 10: The Search Begins 34

Chapter 11: Three Dates 37

Chapter 12: First Sighting 41

Chapter 13: A Terrible Disappointment 45

Chapter 14: Hurt Feelings 49

Chapter 15: Watch Out, Tala! 51

Chapter 16: Critical Condition 54

Chapter 17: Waiting 57

Chapter 18: Relief 60

Chapter 19: A Lunch Shared 64

Chapter 20: New Love 67

Chapter 21: Tala Comes Home 70

Chapter 22: Back to Work 73

Chapter 23: A Funny Misunderstanding 76

Chapter 24: Medical Match 80

Exercises 84

Glossary 87

Answer key 94

Chapter 1

CD1

Gloria Navarro: RN

Gloria pushed her chair away from the dining room table and stood up. Before she could pick up her empty plate, her mother, Tala, took it away for her. "Thanks for dinner, Mom," said Gloria. "It was really good." Then Gloria walked over to the sofa and sat down heavily. "Ugh," she said. "I'm *so* tired!" She stared blankly at the TV screen. "Do you need help with the dishes?" she asked, hoping that her mother didn't need any.

"I'm almost finished in here," answered Tala. "You relax."

Gloria removed the elastic band from around her long, dark ponytail and put her feet up on the sofa. She was happy to relax. She had just finished a ten-hour shift at Riverview General Hospital. As a registered nurse (RN)[+], Gloria was on her feet all day. She had a lot of responsibilities: taking care of patients[+], keeping detailed records, assisting doctors, giving instructions to other nurses, and, of course, supporting patients' families. At the end of her shift, she was totally exhausted.

Becoming a nurse was a long process. Gloria had spent four years in college. Her nursing program was difficult, and she had to study hard. College was also very expensive. Tala, a widow*, had borrowed a lot of money and worked two jobs to help Gloria pay for it. Today, Gloria appreciated that she had a rewarding career with a good salary*. She had been at Riverview General Hospital for the past five years. She was also glad to help support her mother; now, Tala had to work only one part-time job. The problem was that

Gloria felt like she had no time or energy for anything—except work.

"What are you watching?" asked Tala, drying her hands on a towel as she came out of the kitchen.

"I have no idea," said Gloria, still looking at the TV without interest. "I can barely keep my eyes open." Gloria glanced at the clock on the living room wall. "It's only 8:30, and I'm falling asleep," she said. "What an exciting life I have!"

"Well, you should go out more often," said Tala. "You need to have fun. Meet people. You're not getting any younger, you know."

Uh-oh. Here was her mother's speech again. Gloria knew it well: *When I was your age, I was married and had you!* Gloria didn't need to hear it again. Not tonight.

"I'm really tired. I think I'll go to bed," said Gloria. "Good night, Mom."

"Just a moment," said Tala. "I have another thing to discuss with you." Gloria rubbed her eyes and then looked at her mother, who was now standing directly in front of the TV.

"Okay," she said. "I'm listening."

"I saw my old friend Riza today. I hadn't seen her in a long time. She went back to the Philippines for a few years to take care of her mother. Do you remember Riza? She certainly remembers you. Well, Riza joined our mahjong* game this afternoon. Eva generally plays with us, but she is sick. I think she has the stomach flu. She was up all night. Poor Eva! Anyway, Riza, who usually plays with another group on Wednesday, came and…"

"And," said Gloria, yawning, "what happened?"

"Well," said her mother, clearing her throat, "apparently

Riza's son, Antonio Castillo, is still single, too." Gloria groaned and covered her eyes with her hands.

"No, Mom," said Gloria.

"No, what?"

"No Antonio."

"Why not?"

"Because he's a horrible person. When I was eight, he squirted ketchup all over me at that big picnic we had with your friends at the lake."

"That's ridiculous. You can't judge Antonio by some silly thing that happened twenty years ago. Riza tells me that he has grown up to be a wonderful young man. Why don't you meet him for coffee sometime? He just got a job at your hospital! He's a ..."

Gloria stood up suddenly and covered her ears. "Not another word, Mom. Sorry, but I'm not interested. I don't care where Antonio works. I don't care *what* he is," she said loudly, frowning and walking toward her bedroom door. "One thing he will *never* be is *my* husband."

Chapter 2

Love Blossoms on the Bus

The next morning, Gloria hurried to the bus stop and caught the Number 12 bus to Riverview General Hospital. As usual the bus was crowded, but she walked down the aisle and found a seat in the back. Gloria was relieved to sit down. She was working another long shift today, so she didn't want to stand all the way to work and then be on her feet for ten hours. She sat down between a young man listening to some music through a pair of earphones and a young woman text-messaging on a smartphone. Gloria removed the paperback book from her purse, opened it, and tried to read. But she kept looking up and thinking about the conversation she'd had with her mother last night.

Gloria felt bad about speaking to her mother the way she had. She loved her mother dearly and didn't want to be rude, but she didn't like it when Tala interfered in her personal life. It was bad enough when her mother wanted her to meet this son or that nephew related to one of her old friends. But Antonio Castillo? Just imagine! Not in a *million* years. Gloria remembered him perfectly. Antonio was probably about twelve when he chased Gloria and attacked her with a plastic ketchup bottle. The result was ketchup all over her face, in her hair, and on her new pink T-shirt. Gloria had cried all the way home. "So," Gloria thought, "he works at Riverview now. I hope it's not in the cafeteria. That man cannot be trusted near any ketchup!"

Gloria tried to go back to her book, but was distracted by the lively conversation that had developed between the young

"Wow. A romance can begin on the Number 12 bus. Who knew?"

man on her left and the young woman on her right. Suddenly, they seemed to become very interested in each other. Gloria sat uncomfortably between them while they chatted and laughed.

Before the young woman got off the bus, the young man gave her his number—which she immediately entered into her phone. "Wow," thought Gloria. "A romance can begin on the Number 12 bus. Who knew?"

She looked around at the other couples on the bus. Where did they meet? Was it at school? Was it at work? She doubted that their mothers had introduced them. Meeting someone had not been easy for Gloria. She had never really had anyone special in her life. Although she had some good friends in nursing school, she'd never had the time for anything serious. At the hospital, she knew many nice people, but most of them were either married or in relationships. Of course, there were a few single men, but in her mind it was *never* a good idea to date a co-worker. If it didn't work out, then things could get very awkward*.

Gloria looked out the bus window. "Still," she thought honestly, "I am a little lonely. Maybe it *is* time for me to try to meet someone." She thought about how she could do that. Meeting people through friends was one idea. She had a good friend, Laura, at work. Laura was a licensed practical nurse (LPN)+, who had suggested months ago that Gloria meet her funny cousin, Daniel. Maybe she should have lunch with him. Why not? Registering with an online dating* site was another way. According to the advertisements, a lot of people were very successful with that. Meeting someone on a bus was, seemingly, a good way, too. Perhaps Gloria's "soul mate*" would appear on the Number 12 bus tomorrow morning. Maybe she needed to carry an electronic device for luck. Anything was possible! But Gloria was absolutely sure that it was *impossible* for her mother and Riza to arrange a good match. Antonio Castillo—of all people. She shook her head in disbelief.

Gloria got off the bus and walked down 54th Street toward Riverview General Hospital. It was a beautiful spring day. The elm trees along the street were growing their new leaves and cheerful yellow daffodils sprang up below them. "Yes," thought Gloria, "meeting someone special could be very nice." Then she looked up at the large building that was directly in front of her. For now, Gloria needed to enter that building, take the elevator to the fifth floor, and do her best to take care of the many people whose lives depended on her. Nothing else was more important.

Chapter 3

An Embarrassing Lie

Gloria stepped onto the fifth floor of Riverview General Hospital. The silly thoughts that had occupied her mind on the bus had completely disappeared. At work she was Gloria Navarro, a highly respected RN. She had earned the admiration of both co-workers and patients for her dedication* and hard work.

Gloria walked directly into the locker room, put on a clean pair of scrubs+, and wrapped a stethoscope+ around her neck. Then she met with Alex, the outgoing nurse, and reviewed his reports from the previous shift. He wanted Gloria to know a lot of different things: "Mrs. Greenstein in Room 517 is still in a lot of pain from her hip-replacement surgery. Please remind the staff to be gentle with her. Joshua Garrett in 524 is improving slightly after a rough skateboarding accident. He's going to be okay, but his mother is very difficult. She sits at his beside during visiting hours and yells at everyone about everything. And Mr. Marino in 520 had some mild complications+ after his gallbladder surgery—a fever+ and some nausea+—but should be able to go home later today."

Gloria and Alex went on their rounds* together. As they entered each room, Alex introduced—or reintroduced—all of the patients to Gloria. She spoke kindly to each one while she read their charts+ and reviewed their medical histories. As an RN, Gloria often had more contact with the patients than their doctors did. She was usually the first person to notice problems and she took this responsibility very seriously.

Gloria returned to the nurse's station and gave instructions to both Laura and Anh, the certified nursing assistant (CNA)⁺. Gloria was fortunate to supervise* two very dependable* nurses who followed Gloria's instructions well. Laura needed to change Joshua Garrett's sterile⁺ dressings⁺. His skateboarding accident had left him with some serious cuts and abrasions⁺, along with three broken bones. Anh needed to carefully bathe Mrs. Greenstein. And Gloria needed to follow all of the doctors' orders, evaluate patients, start IVs⁺, hand out medications⁺, and accomplish* a wide range of other tasks for the next ten hours.

At 6:30p.m., Gloria got back on the Number 12 bus. Her feet hurt, but she felt good about her day at work. In addition to being a hardworking RN, Gloria had an excellent bedside manner*. She had helped Mr. Marino get ready to leave the hospital, giving him clear instructions about his post-operative diet⁺. She also warned him not to do too much once he returned home. "Walking is good," she said, "but don't lift anything heavier than a gallon of milk for two weeks."

Mr. Marino appreciated Gloria's attention. "Thank you so much for your excellent care," he said, as Gloria helped him into the wheelchair⁺ before he was discharged⁺. Then he shook her hand warmly. "You were wonderful."

Gloria also had a very calming effect on Joshua Garrett's mother. Of course, she was upset about her son's skateboarding accident. Gloria knew that some people could be unpleasant in stressful situations. It was true that Mrs. Garrett had yelled at several people on the hospital staff: "I don't like the view from this room! I want my son in another one! The mashed potatoes on this lunch tray look just awful! My dog wouldn't eat them!" But Gloria always seemed to know how to comfort people like Mrs Garrett.

"Actually, this is the best room on the floor, Mrs. Garrett. It's right by my station, so Joshua will always come first on my rounds. But you're right about the mashed potatoes. They don't look very good today. I'll bring him something else." Mrs. Garrett calmed down instantly and looked at Gloria.

"Thank you," she said. "*Finally* there is someone in this place who listens to me and…please, call me *Julia*."

There was really only one incident today that bothered Gloria, and that was her strange conversation with Mrs. Greenstein in Room 517. Gloria had gone to her room late in the afternoon to help her change positions in bed. Mrs. Greenstein had recently taken her pain medication and seemed very comfortable. "You're a lovely young woman," she said affectionately*. "Are you married?"

"No, I'm not," Gloria answered politely.

"Well, I think you might be just the girl for my grandson, Larry. He's a darling young man. But he's very shy. Not good with girls at all. Would it be okay for him to call you sometime?" asked Mrs. Greenstein, smiling dreamily from her pillow. Gloria quickly looked down at Mrs. Greenstein's chart and tried desperately to think of an excuse—for her sake and for Larry's.

"Uh, well," she said hesitantly, "I'm not married *yet*. But I am engaged."

"Oh, really?" asked Mrs. Greenstein, curiously. "You have a fiancé! Congratulations! How nice! So, what's the lucky man's name?" Gloria felt a pain in her stomach. *His name?* She didn't want to tell a lie. But Mrs. Greenstein had just taken her pain medication, so she probably wouldn't even remember this conversation tomorrow. Gloria desperately tried to think of a name—any name in the world.

"It's, uh…it's, um…Antonio Castillo."

Chapter 4

A Friend Offended

Tala worked part time as a home health aide*. She took care of Mr. and Mrs. Campbell, an elderly couple who lived in her neighborhood. Mr. and Mrs. Campbell, ages 94 and 89, had lived in the same house for nearly sixty years and didn't want to move. Because their children and grandchildren lived a few hours away in another city, they employed Tala and three other caregivers, Sophia, Wanda, and Dora, to assist them. When Tala went to the Campbells' home, she generally focused on Mr. Campbell, who required more care. She helped him with basic tasks, like bathing and dressing. She assisted him with simple exercises and brought him his medication⁺ at the right times. She also prepared meals and did some light housekeeping. Tala had worked for the Campbells for over three years, and their whole family was grateful for her kindness and dependability.

During the day, Mr. Campbell slept a lot in front of the TV. But Mrs. Campbell really enjoyed Tala's conversation. Mrs. Campbell had heard many stories about Tala growing up in the Philippines. She knew that Tala had immigrated* to the U.S., where Gloria was born. She knew that her husband had died after a long illness when Gloria was only eight years old, and that Tala had struggled financially for many years—until Gloria got her nursing job at Riverview General Hospital. And she knew that while Tala was extremely proud of her daughter, she also wanted her to have a happy life. Of course, a good job was important. But, according to Tala, a husband

and a family were also very important. "Has she met anyone at that hospital yet?" asked Mrs. Campbell.

"Not yet," Tala sighed. "And she doesn't want my advice."

"Maybe she's waiting for a handsome* stranger to enter her life," laughed Mrs. Campbell, who often asked Tala to read romance novels aloud to her.

"Well," said Tala, "a handsome stranger won't just appear in real life. And she definitely won't find one in a hospital room. I just offered to introduce her to a nice man from a good family, but she won't listen to me."

Tala left the Campbells' home when Wanda arrived at 6:00p.m. It was a beautiful spring evening, but Tala felt a little sad as she walked down the street. She dreaded* having to call Riza when she got home. How could she explain that Gloria wasn't interested in meeting her son? There was no way to say that without hurting Riza's feelings—and Antonio's too.

Tala unlocked the front door. She gathered up the mail and put it on the table in the entryway. There was the gas and electric bill again. Before Gloria got her full-time job, Tala used to worry about how she was going to pay it—and all the other bills—every month. Tala walked into the kitchen and turned on the light. She remembered a few times in the past when the lights hadn't come on because she couldn't pay that bill. Now, Tala was grateful to have the support of a generous daughter. Yes, she was a little disappointed about the Antonio situation. But she decided to make something delicious for Gloria when she got home. Her daughter had a very demanding job and needed to stay strong and healthy. It was bad enough that she ate a lot of her meals in the hospital cafeteria.

Tala opened her refrigerator and took out the chicken, carrots, celery, onions, and garlic. Then she opened the cabinet and took out the rice noodles, oil, soy sauce, and pepper.

She planned to make a delicious stir-fry meal with these ingredients. Gloria would enjoy it when she got home. Before she removed the wok from the shelf, though, Tala opened a drawer in the kitchen. She reached in and took out her old address book with the daisies on the cover. Tala couldn't enjoy cooking—or eating—until she called Riza to apologize. It was a mistake to assume that Gloria would be interested in Antonio. Tala wished that she and Riza had never discussed it.

Tala dialed Riza's number and felt her heart beating very hard in her chest. Riza answered on the third ring. "Hello?"

"Good evening, Riza," she said. "This is Tala. I hope everything is going well with you today."

"Yes," said Riza. "Everything is fine, thank you."

"Well," continued Tala, nervously, "I'm calling about my daughter. I'm sorry, but she doesn't really want to go out with Antonio."

"Why not?" asked Riza, in a very surprised voice. "Does she think she's too good for him?"

"Oh, no!" answered Tala. "That's not it. You know how young people are today. They're very independent. They don't want their mothers to interfere in their lives."

"My son is a good man, Tala," said Riza. "Many women would love to meet a man like Antonio. Don't forget, he is a *doctor* at Riverview General Hospital. You daughter would be lucky to find a man like him."

"Yes, I know," continued Tala, uncomfortably. "I feel very embarrassed about this. If you wish, I can call Antonio and tell him how sorry I am."

"That isn't necessary," answered Riza. "I talked to him about your daughter last night, and…and…"

"And what did he say?" asked Tala.

"Um, he doesn't want to meet her either."

Chapter 5

CD1
5

Antonio's Story

It was true that Antonio Castillo worked at Riverview General Hospital. He was an anesthesiologist, a doctor who prevented patients from feeling pain during surgeries. Antonio had worked extremely hard to earn this position: four years at university, four years in medical school, and another four years of specialized* training. He had worked at a different hospital for two years before joining the staff at Riverview General Hospital just a few weeks ago.

Antonio worked in several areas of the hospital. Sometimes he was in a patient's room having a pre-operative interview. At that time, he reviewed the patient's medical history, discussed his or her upcoming surgical procedure+, and talked about options for anesthesia—pain-killing drugs. He also spent many hours in operating rooms. During surgeries, Antonio carefully checked a patient's vital signs— heart rate, blood pressure, breathing, and kidney function— and adjusted the medicines when necessary. Then he went to the post-operation recovery+ rooms and monitored his patients while the effects of the anesthesia wore off.

As a member of a surgical team of doctors and nurses, Antonio's job could be very stressful. He had to be calm during life-and-death situations and pay extremely close attention during lengthy medical procedures. He worked very long hours and was also on call a lot of the time. That meant that if there was an emergency+, Antonio had to rush to the hospital, day or night, to assist in the operating room.

It wasn't really surprising that Antonio and Gloria had never met each other. For one thing, the operating rooms were not on the fifth floor, where Gloria worked. Although Antonio often talked with doctors, nurses, and patients all over Riverview General Hospital—including ones on the fifth floor—their paths simply hadn't crossed. Perhaps Antonio and Gloria had been too preoccupied* with their own patients to notice one another. Or perhaps Antonio was working when Gloria wasn't. Certainly, in Gloria's case, she hadn't given the fact that Antonio worked *somewhere* at Riverview General Hospital another thought. Well, perhaps she did mention his *name* to Mrs. Greenstein, but that was only because she couldn't think of another one. And like Gloria the evening before, Antonio also became irritated when he returned his mother's call: "Who? *Gloria Navarro?* Well, I *might* remember her. A nurse at this hospital? No, I haven't seen her. No, I don't need to meet her. No, Mom. That probably isn't a good idea. I really don't have time for that. Really busy here, Mom. Sorry, but I have to go."

Three days later, Antonio was on the fifth floor to see a patient. As he walked by Room 517, he noticed Mrs. Greenstein sitting up in bed. Antonio remembered meeting her five days ago. He had been the anesthesiologist during her hip-replacement surgery. He understood that she was doing very well and would be going home in the morning. Antonio walked into her room. "Good evening, Mrs. Greenstein. I'm Dr. Castillo, your anesthesiologist. We met before your surgery. How are you feeling?" he asked, kindly.

"Much better!" said Mrs. Greenstein, cheerfully. "Yes, I remember you. This hip is almost as good as new."

"So," continued Antonio. "I hear that you're leaving in the morning. I wish you the best of luck with your recovery."

"Thank you," said Mrs. Greenstein. "I've been cared for so well here. And during my surgery, I didn't feel a thing! I sincerely* appreciate everything you did for me."

"You're very welcome," said Antonio. "And don't forget: No driving for six weeks. Remember to schedule your follow-up appointments⁺. And please attend all of your physical therapy⁺ sessions. That will help a lot."

Mrs. Greenstein pointed to a pile of paper on her nightstand. "Thanks, Doctor Castillo. You can see that they're sending me home with pages and pages of instructions. How can I forget?" She smiled at Dr. Castillo. "But there is one thing I have forgotten: your *first* name."

"Oh, it's *Antonio*," he replied.

"Well, how about that? *You're* Antonio Castillo!" laughed Mrs. Greenstein. "Your fiancée has been taking very good care of me this week!" Antonio looked confused.

"I think you must be mistaking me for someone else. I'm definitely not engaged. In fact, I am quite single."

"You're not? Uh, you are? Oh, dear. Now I feel very foolish. I suppose my nurse was referring to another *Antonio Castillo*. I imagine there are other people in the world with that name. Sorry about that."

"That's okay," laughed Antonio. "But you had me worried for a minute. Had I forgotten to put my own wedding day on the calendar? And, for goodness sake, *who* was I going to marry?"

Chapter 6

A Day Off for Gloria

Gloria had the day off on Saturday. In the morning, she put on her running shoes and ran for nearly five miles on the jogging path along the river. Because her job was very physically, mentally, and emotionally demanding, Gloria really tried to exercise when she had the time. Running helped her to relax and put things in perspective*. Halfway through her run, she could see Riverview General Hospital up on the hill. She really didn't want to imagine what was happening inside that building when she wasn't there. A day off gave her a much-needed break from all of the responsibility and real-life drama.

Yesterday one of her patients, Mr. Padilla, died after having a cardiac arrest⁺. His heart was being monitored at all times, especially because he had a history of serious cardiac problems. So when an alarm sounded in his room indicating a possible heart attack, Gloria was the first to respond. She shouted for help and began cardiopulmonary resuscitation (CPR)⁺. Within seconds, a team had gathered with oxygen, medicines, and a defibrillator—an electrical device that restored the heart's normal rhythm. They tried everything to save Mr. Padilla, but, unfortunately, they couldn't. He was a very nice man with a lovely family. And they were grief-stricken when they gathered together afterwards in his room. Of course, these things sometimes happened in a hospital, but it was never easy to accept them.

After a day like this, Gloria often felt very upset after work. She was greatly affected by all the pain and suffering she saw at Riverview General Hospital. So on her early morning run, she really tried to clear her mind and focus on other things. Actually, there was something to look forward to later today. She had finally agreed to go out to lunch with Laura and her cousin, Daniel. She wasn't nervous about it. And she certainly didn't expect Daniel to be her "soul mate." But Gloria thought that meeting him couldn't hurt. "Why not meet him and see what you think?" said Laura on the telephone the night before. "He's totally different from you. But sometimes, you know, opposites attract."

Later that morning, Gloria took care of a few errands at the nearby shopping mall. First, she withdrew $200 at an ATM. Then she went into the bookstore and found the book that Tala had asked her to buy for Mrs. Campbell: *Passion on the Highlands*. "Can you imagine?" said Gloria to herself, looking at the cover. "Almost ninety years old, and she loves this stuff!" Gloria read the description on the back cover: *Tall, handsome Colin meets Abbie, a beautiful but spirited red-haired lass from another Scottish clan. Will their warring families tear them apart?* Gloria laughed out loud. "I suppose warring families could be a challenge in any relationship," she thought. Gloria didn't want anyone to see her carrying this book, so she quietly asked the cashier to put it in a bag.

A few minutes later, Gloria saw a pretty pair of black sandals in a store window. She walked inside, tried them on, and bought them. She almost never bought things on impulse* but was trying to be more spontaneous*. "I've paid the bills this month. And I haven't bought anything new for a long time," she reasoned to herself. "And I need these because neither my running shoes nor my work shoes match my outfit." Then she gathered up the new sandals and the romance novel and headed home.

*Gloria was dressed
in a pretty blue
skirt, a white
sweater, and the
new black sandals.*

At noon, Tala walked by Gloria's bedroom and saw her daughter brushing her hair in front of the mirror. She was dressed in a pretty blue skirt, a white sweater, and the new black sandals.

Tala knew this wasn't the way that Gloria usually looked on her day off. Last Saturday she had stayed in her running clothes and spent the whole afternoon reading on the sofa. Tala smiled with approval. While she didn't need to know every detail of her twenty-eight-year-old daughter's life, she was still very curious. "Going out?" Tala asked casually.

"Yes, Mom," replied Gloria. "Just lunch with some friends."

"Well, you look very nice," commented Tala. And she meant it. Gloria was a beautiful young woman, and Tala was extremely proud of her. She was happy to see her going out and enjoying life a little. "Have a good time." Tala turned toward the kitchen. "Who knows?" she thought to herself. "Maybe she did meet a handsome stranger at that hospital. I can't wait to share this exciting news with Mrs. Campbell!"

Chapter 7

A Disastrous Date

When Gloria arrived at *Giorgio's* Italian restaurant on Market Street, Laura and Daniel were already waiting for her at the entrance. Before they arranged this lunch, Gloria had insisted that Laura join them. Blind dates* were, in Gloria's opinion, a lot of pressure. It would be easier to have Laura there. Laura knew both Gloria and Daniel very well and could help make the conversation a little easier, especially if they had very little in common.

Gloria had wanted this lunch date to be very informal. Still, Laura was dressed in a pair of nice pants and a pretty blouse. Daniel, on the other hand, was definitely underdressed. He was in a football jersey and torn jeans. He wore a backwards baseball cap on his head and old flip–flops on his feet. But he gave Gloria a warm smile, shook her hand, and was very friendly.

The server at the restaurant brought them water and menus. "I hear that the food is really good here," said Daniel. "Ladies, please order whatever you want." Gloria hadn't expected Daniel to pay for her lunch but, before she could say anything, he had already turned to Laura and whispered, "Hey, cousin. Can I please borrow a few bucks? My mom didn't have any extra cash this morning, so I'm a little short." Gloria felt a wave of embarrassment as Laura took twenty dollars out of her purse and handed it to Daniel. "Maybe another twenty?" asked Daniel even more quietly. "Then I won't worry when the bill comes." Laura pulled another twenty dollars out of her purse and slipped it into Daniel's hand. Gloria looked away and pretended to be interested in the décor of the restaurant.

Once Daniel had Laura's money in his wallet, Gloria said, "I hear that you work in construction*."

"Well, I do when there *is* work," answered Daniel. "But right now it's a little slow, so I'm living in my mom's basement and eating her delicious food."

Gloria didn't necessarily think that this was a bad thing. After all, she lived with her mother—and ate *her* mother's delicious food. And she knew how it felt to be unemployed* and dependent on other people.

"I see. Where were you living before you moved home?" she asked, smoothing out the napkin on her lap.

"Oh, no. I've never lived away from home. My mom has been lucky to take care of me for the last thirty-one years! But it's all good. She likes cooking for me and doing my laundry. I think it gives her something to do," Daniel said with a smile, grabbing a piece of garlic bread before the server had a chance to place the basket on the table.

During lunch, Daniel talked a lot. He pointed out several of the tattoos on his arms and explained their meanings. "This one here," he said, putting his right forearm on the table, "is the broken heart my last girlfriend gave me. And this scorpion* on my left arm represents the pain I went through with the girlfriend before that. And this one here is supposed to mean *Love* in Chinese. But when I showed it to an actual Chinese guy, he told me that it really meant *Stupidity.*"

"Oh," said Gloria. "Well, I would never have known that."

By the time lunch was over, Gloria definitely knew that Daniel, even with his easygoing* attitude and ready smile, was not the person who was missing in her life. Daniel seemed very immature* for a thirty-one-year-old man.

"This scorpion on my left arm represents the pain I went through."

He didn't have any goals and seemed perfectly content not doing anything—except for, perhaps, adding more tattoos to his body. Daniel never once asked Gloria any questions about herself. He did express some curiosity about the annual salaries of nurses, but Gloria and Laura managed to change the subject. Supporting Daniel financially, cooking, and doing his laundry for the *next* thirty-one years did not appeal to Gloria whatsoever. She would gladly leave that responsibility to his mother.

Gloria, Laura, and Daniel left the restaurant at about 3:00p.m. and walked down Market Street together. They'd had a good meal, but Gloria thought that she had probably seen Daniel for the last time. They all stopped for a moment in front of a movie theater. "How about we all see a movie?" Daniel asked enthusiastically. "It looks like we can catch the next showing at 3:30." Then Daniel looked into his wallet. "But I've spent most of *my* money at the restaurant. Hey, Gloria. We're old friends now. Can I please borrow a few bucks?"

Chapter 8

A Life Saved

On Monday morning, Gloria saw Laura in the locker room before their shifts began. "Sorry about lunch with Daniel," said Laura, apologetically. "He's my cousin, so I see the good in him. And he has a lot of *potential**. But he probably isn't right for you. I mean…"

"Don't worry about it," laughed Gloria, pressing twenty dollars into Laura's hand. "Please take this for my half of that very interesting lunch. Besides, it's good for me to go out and meet new people. Daniel is a very amusing guy, but I don't think there's enough room on his arm for a *Gloria* tattoo—or the painful symbol of our breakup*."

"He might be able to squeeze it in, but he couldn't afford it without borrowing the money from you." They both laughed and walked onto the fifth floor to begin their shifts.

On her morning rounds, Gloria looked at Joshua Garrett in Room 524 with concern. Joshua was the teenage boy who had been in a serious skateboarding accident. Although his injuries hadn't allowed him to be discharged from the hospital just yet, Joshua was usually awake and talkative in the morning. Today, however, he was groaning and shivering under his bed sheet. Gloria took his temperature: 102 degrees. She took his blood pressure, and it was lower than it should have been. Gloria put on a pair of latex* gloves and removed a dressing on Joshua's right leg. She observed that the area around the wound⁺ was very red and swollen.

Gloria feared that Joshua had developed a staphylococcal (staph) infection that may have entered his body through the many deep cuts he had from the accident. Unfortunately, these types of infections occurred often in patients in hospitals. When a staph infection entered the bloodstream, it could quickly spread to other internal organs[+]. And if left untreated, a staph infection could be fatal[+].

According to his chart, Joshua had been taking antibiotics[+] to fight infection, but they were clearly not working now. Unfortunately, some varieties of staph bacteria had become resistant to different types of antibiotics. It was time to start a more aggressive treatment immediately. Gloria quickly summoned Dr. Nguyen, who she had just seen on the fifth floor. Dr. Nguyen completely agreed with her assessment. Within minutes, Joshua was receiving a stronger antibiotic through an IV line that Gloria skillfully connected.

Over the next several hours, Joshua slowly improved. His temperature went down, and his blood pressure went up. The areas around his wounds became less swollen. When Mrs. Garrett came in at visiting hours, she was very surprised to find Dr. Nguyen and Gloria examining Joshua in his hospital room. "What's going on?" Mrs. Garrett asked loudly. "What's happening to my son?"

"Your son is being treated with a strong IV antibiotic after having a serious setback* from a staph infection," said Dr. Nguyen. "The early lab test results have confirmed it. We tried to reach you, but you didn't respond."

"I'm so sorry! I guess my cell phone was turned off. How did *this* happen?"

Dr. Nguyen explained the ways that staph infections could occur. Then she added, "The important thing is that your son's nurse, Gloria Navarro, identified the problem immediately—and may have saved his life."

"Oh, my gosh! Thank you so much!" said Mrs. Garrett.

"Don't mention it, Julia," said Gloria. "And Joshua is feeling better already. He just told us that he felt hungry."

"Yeah, I do," said Joshua, weakly. "When you have a minute, I would love a plate of those mashed potatoes."

After making sure that Joshua got his meal—with extra mashed potatoes—Gloria went down to the hospital cafeteria for her own dinner break. She had told Tala this morning that she would be working later than usual. But before taking the elevator down to the first floor, Gloria stopped in the locker room and pulled a book out of her backpack. It was *Passion on the Highlands*. Gloria had picked it up at home last night, and surprisingly enough, she couldn't put it down. Today was Tala's day off. If Gloria read a little more now, she could probably finish it tonight, just in time to for Tala to bring it to Mrs. Campbell in the morning.

Gloria put a salad, a bowl of soup, and some juice on her tray. Then she wandered over to the far side of the dining room and found a seat away from everyone else. She was embarrassed to be reading a romance novel and didn't want any of her co-workers to see her.

Twenty minutes later, Gloria was fully engrossed* in the story, her food only half-eaten. She had gotten to an exciting part: Colin had just saved Abbie's father's life in a fierce battle. And even though Abbie's father had once been his own father's enemy, perhaps now Colin could ask for Abbie's hand.

"Excuse me," said a voice behind Gloria. "May I use your ketchup?"

"Yes, of course," said Gloria, absently. And without removing her eyes from the page, she handed the bottle to a person who sat at the table directly behind her. She had absolutely no idea that it was Dr. Antonio Castillo's hand that accepted it or his voice that said, "Thank you."

"Excuse me. May I use your ketchup?"

Chapter 9

CD1

Ketchup Required

At 6:00p.m., Antonio was also taking his dinner break. He had just spent three hours in surgery and needed to stay at the hospital until at least midnight. Other than the occasionally very late hours, Antonio really liked his position at Riverview General Hospital. Still, as with any new job, he hadn't formed any strong friendships yet. It took time to develop relationships with co-workers, and he was still in the process of getting to know a very large group of people.

Antonio was the youngest child of Riza and Danilo Castillo. Antonio and his three older sisters were born and raised in the U.S. However, because their parents were originally from the Philippines, the Castillo family went back every few years for a visit. Riza and Danilo had recently come back from living in the Philippines for a while. Riza's mother was elderly and needed a lot of care. Their grown children were managing well in the U.S., so Riza and Danilo stayed in the Philippines with Riza's mother until she died the previous June.

Riza and Danilo were happy to be living closer to their four children—and seven grandchildren—once again. Luckily, their daughters and their families lived relatively close. But Riza was especially happy to be nearer to Antonio, who was, and would always be, her baby. For Riza, it was very fortunate that Antonio had found his way back to the city where he grew up. And better yet, he lived in an apartment that was only ten minutes away from her home. Frankly, Riza would have been even happier if Antonio lived with her. After all, that's the way many families lived in the Philippines. It was Antonio's choice to have a little distance from his parents. Although he saw them at least once a week, he really needed the privacy when he wasn't working.

Antonio had also received some pressure from his mother to find a suitable, preferably Filipina, woman and settle down. In Riza's opinion, he needed someone to take care of him. It was, perhaps, an old-fashioned* view, but that's the way she saw it. In the months since Riza had returned from the Philippines, she had dutifully* pointed out various daughters, nieces, and granddaughters from among her circle of friends. It was obvious that some young women had been invited to various family functions just to meet him: "Antonio, this is Raina. She works in the bank on 7th Avenue. Isn't that nice?" In most cases, however, these meetings were as awkward for him as they were for the young women.

Although Antonio had dated a few women over the years, he didn't have any tattoos to remember them by. And none of them had ever felt like "the one." Also, relationships often took time and, as a doctor, Antonio had very little of that. Many people didn't understand the demands of his job: the long hours and the telephone calls that interrupted movies and meals in restaurants. Still, Antonio had no regrets about choosing his profession. From a very young age, he was determined to become a doctor and help people. Having pursued his dream for twelve years, he couldn't imagine letting it go just so he could go out more often.

On his days off, Antonio took care of his personal business the same way everyone did. He went grocery shopping. He did the laundry. He paid his bills. He worked out at the local gym. He watched some sports on TV. And, of course, he dutifully visited his parents. Naturally there were some lonely moments, but his job was definitely his main focus. He really didn't have the time or energy to worry too much about his own life.

Antonio looked around the crowded cafeteria for a place to sit. He noticed a pretty young woman wearing hospital scrubs reading along the far wall. Antonio was almost sure that he hadn't met her at the hospital, although something about her looked vaguely* familiar. He wondered where she worked. He had met most of the surgeons. Was she a doctor or a nurse? Perhaps she worked in the lab*. In any event, she was completely absorbed in her book and didn't look up as he approached.

Antonio placed his tray on a table near hers. Then he took a seat, so that they were back-to-back. He thought about leaning over and starting a conversation with her. He didn't want to be too forward, but he would have liked to chat for a few minutes. For a moment, he turned around. He almost asked what she was reading, but decided not to interrupt. Maybe she really needed this break and didn't want to talk to anyone. Antonio understood that feeling very well. Still, he would have liked to introduce himself. And why did he feel that he knew her? "Well," he thought. "I could use some ketchup and there is a bottle on her table."

Upon his request, Gloria managed to pass Antonio the ketchup without meeting his eyes for a second. She spoke only two syllables in response to his words of thanks: "Uh-huh."

Antonio squirted a little ketchup onto his French fries. "Oh, well," he said to himself. "I can't compete with that book for her attention, so I won't even try."

Chapter 10

The Search Begins

Gloria stood up, gathered her things, and walked toward the area where she could return her tray. She looked straight ahead and not back at Antonio, who was still studying—and admiring—her. *Where* had he seen this woman before? The thought actually began to torment* him. Perhaps, if he caught up with her at the elevator, *she* would remember *him*. Antonio thought about following her out the door, but didn't want to be considered desperate—or silly. *Excuse me. Don't I know you from someplace?* The question sounded so phony*. If he only knew her name, he could perhaps remember. Antonio felt a little sad to see the glass doors of the cafeteria close behind her. He sighed and took a bite of his sandwich. The chances of running into her again in this huge hospital were not very good.

Gloria left work at 10:00p.m., and Tala was happy when she made it home safely at 10:30. She never liked to think of her daughter out alone late at night. Fortunately, she didn't have to take the bus home this time. Anh, one of the CNAs on the fifth floor, lived nearby. As they both got off work at the same time tonight, Anh had kindly offered to drive Gloria home. Now Tala could go to bed without worrying about her.

Gloria, however, didn't go straight to bed. She made herself a strong cup of tea and plopped down on the sofa to finish the last few chapters of *Passion on the Highlands*. Within a half-hour, she had finished it. Although Gloria was quite sure that *Passion on the Highlands* was not going to

34

win any literary awards, she had to admit that it was very entertaining. Of course, everything had turned out well for Colin and Abbie. The battles were won. Their families had made peace. They were perfectly free to be in love and live *happily ever after* in fifteenth-century Scotland.

If she was honest with herself, Gloria felt a little envious*. There were times that she was very doubtful that she would ever find true love. A lot of her childhood friends were already married. Gloria thought about her lunch date with Daniel. "Ridiculous," she thought. "There was no chemistry* at all." Gloria closed her eyes for a moment. Who were the other men in her life? Well, Joshua Garrett was one, but he was about fifteen years too young. Gloria laughed to imagine a skateboarding date, and having to follow him around with sterile bandages and an IV.

She got up from the sofa and placed *Passion on the Highlands* next to Tala's purse. Tomorrow her mother could begin reading it to Mrs. Campbell, who would definitely enjoy it. Then Gloria wandered into her bedroom and turned on her laptop computer. It was very late, but working a lot of overtime had earned her another day off tomorrow. Besides, she still felt wide-awake from the tea. So she logged onto the Internet and explored some dating websites. She did feel a little uncomfortable about using this method to meet someone, but she had heard that a lot of modern relationships began this way. Dr. Nguyen at the hospital had once told her that she met her husband online.

Gloria was intrigued* as she looked at the many photos of men, between the ages of 25 and 35, in her area. Some of them were actually very good-looking. "Perhaps the right guy for me is one of them," she thought. "But I won't know unless I try." So as part of her effort to be more spontaneous,

Gloria began the sign-up process. She filled out a profile including information about her height, body type, marital status, ethnicity, religion, education, and other details. She answered several other questions about her hobbies, interests, lifestyle, values, and what she was looking for in a partner. Gloria suspected that her answers to some of these questions would dramatically reduce the possibilities, but hopefully they could match her up with someone.

Gloria found it easy to describe herself. It was the answers about who she was looking *for* that were not as simple. Someone attractive would be nice, if possible. She also preferred tall, athletic, and never married. She wasn't particular about dating a Filipino-American. Thank goodness Tala wasn't helping her with this profile, or she probably would have indicated that preference. "It's easier when a couple shares the same culture," her mother often said. Gloria, on the other hand, was quite open-minded*. The only type she was *not* looking for was a happily unemployed man who was completely dependent on his mother. She wanted to make sure that she would never be matched up with a person like Daniel.

Gloria had a long, wonderful sleep. When she woke up, she checked her account. There were already five matches. "Incredible!" she gasped. "Perhaps love will be easier to find than I had imagined!"

Chapter 11

CD1

Three Dates

For the next three weeks, Gloria explored the world of online dating. She exchanged a few e-mail messages with her first "match." But she soon decided that they were probably incompatible*. Right away, this person informed Gloria that he was a huge sports fan. He claimed to watch hours and hours of sporting events on TV each week. He insisted that a future girlfriend would have to share this hobby. Gloria, however, had neither the time nor the interest to spend hours and hours watching sports, so she quickly decided that they had no future. The second "match" also never made it beyond the e-mail stage. This person admitted to dating several women at the same time and was, little by little, "eliminating* them." Gloria really didn't like the way that sounded and so, after a few e-mail messages, *she* eliminated *him*. However, she met the last three "matches" in person: one in a coffee shop, one in the park, and one in a Chinese restaurant for dinner.

She met Tyler in a coffee shop one morning on her day off. He was twenty-eight, tall, blonde, and very good-looking. Tyler talked a lot about himself. While Gloria sipped her tea, she learned that he worked in a restaurant. His real dream, though, was to pursue modeling and acting. Apparently, he had recently appeared in some advertisements for a local clothing store. He proudly pulled a newspaper clipping out of his wallet, unfolded it, and passed it across the table to Gloria. Sure enough, there was Tyler modeling a dress shirt and tie, looking just like a corporate executive. "Wow," said Gloria. "That must be very exciting for you."

"Oh, definitely. Next I'll go after the bigger projects. You know, movie roles and so on. I have it all planned out," he said, turning toward the mirror on the wall and smiling at his reflection. Once, Gloria attempted to talk about her work, but Tyler seemed to lose interest immediately. "Gross," he said. "I hate hospitals. Too many sick people."

Gloria refused a refill of her tea and politely said, "Well, nice meeting you, Tyler! I have to run! Good luck with your career!" She'd had enough of Tyler. She greatly preferred the image he projected in the newspaper ad to the real person.

A week later, Gloria had another first date. This time it was with Joseph, a twenty-five-year-old lab technician who worked at another hospital. Joseph suggested that they meet in a dog-friendly area of the park, so Gloria could also meet his dog—and "best friend"—Boomer. Gloria had never owned a pet, but she usually liked dogs a lot.

"I think Boomer just isn't ready for a serious relationship."

Boomer, however, may have been the one dog in the world she didn't like. When Gloria shook hands with Joseph, Boomer growled at her. When they sat on the park bench Boomer sat between them, barking constantly and making conversation almost impossible. When Gloria attempted to gently pet Boomer, the dog bared his teeth, prompting Gloria to jump up and move several feet away. After a very awkward twenty minutes, Joseph announced, "No offense, Gloria, you seem like a nice person, but you and I probably aren't going to work out. I think Boomer just isn't ready for a serious relationship."

Because Gloria's two other dates had gone so poorly, she almost canceled the third one. But since the plans were in place, she proceeded to meet Armando, a thirty-three-year-old medical equipment salesman, at a Chinese restaurant downtown. At first, Gloria hoped that this date might be okay. Armando was nicely dressed and had a respectable job. He did not admire himself in a mirror or keep a vicious dog under the table. But there was one problem: Armando quickly revealed that a recent girlfriend had just broken his heart. Gloria would have preferred not to hear about it, but there was no stopping Armando's long, sad story. By the time their meals had arrived, Gloria had heard more than she ever wanted to about his previous relationship. It had left him very depressed and doubtful that he could "ever find love again." At this point, Gloria had to pass Armando a second napkin to dry his tears.

After their meal, Armando offered to call Gloria sometime, but she refused. "I think you need time to heal from this experience," she said, kindly. They shook hands at the bus stop, and Armando disappeared down the street.

After five minutes, the bus pulled up to Gloria's stop. She got onto the bus, sat in an empty seat, and hung her head. After reflecting on one dating disaster after another, she was now in a horrible mood. Online dating had been a major disappointment. She had found a sports fanatic and a womanizer*. She had found a narcissist* and a person who valued the feelings of a jealous dog more than her own. And she had found someone hopelessly in love with another person. If these were her "matches," Gloria would *hate* to see the people who weren't right for her. At that moment, Gloria decided to stop trying to be spontaneous. Her attempts to meet new people had just been a waste of time and energy. Real life wasn't at all like a romance novel.

Chapter 12

First Sighting

Work helped Gloria keep her mind off of her recent bad luck in the dating world. Fortunately, there was one very happy event that occurred shortly after Gloria's awful date with Armando: Joshua Garrett was finally well enough to leave the hospital. He made a solemn* promise to never again ride his skateboard on a narrow ledge, high above a pile of rocks. And he promised to always wear protective clothing and a helmet. "Don't worry," said his mother, as Gloria and Laura gently helped Joshua into his wheelchair. "He won't be riding that horrible thing ever again."

"Yes," said Joshua in agreement. "I don't really think I'll need it anymore. Besides, I'm almost old enough to ride a motorcycle."

"A *motorcycle*?" shrieked Julia. "Do you want to live in this hospital permanently?" Laura laughed and waved good-bye to the Garretts. Then Gloria received the most heartfelt hug from Julia Garrett. "Thank you so much for everything you did," she said softly, her voice cracking with emotion. "You are an amazing nurse—and an amazing person." Then she pulled a small box out of her purse and handed it to Gloria.

"Oh, you didn't have to do that!" exclaimed Gloria, looking at Joshua and Mrs. Garrett in surprise.

"We know," said Julia. "But we wanted to. Please open it." Gloria opened the box and inside was a beautiful silver bracelet with three lovely charms on it: a heart, a medical symbol, and a skateboard.

"My mom thought it would suit you, but the skateboard was my idea," said Joshua, "so you won't forget me."

Gloria took the lovely piece of jewelry out of the box, examined it closely, and then slipped it around her wrist.

"It's just beautiful. Thank you so much. And I will *never* forget you."

"Well, that accident was really scary. I wasn't sure that I was ever going to get better," Joshua said, wiping away the tears that had formed in his eyes. "And then there was the staph infection. I was afraid I was going to die. Thanks a lot for helping to save my life."

At that moment, Gloria felt her heart overflow with love. She bent down over Joshua's wheelchair and hugged him gently.

"What more could a person possibly want out of life?" thought Gloria. She was so grateful for the opportunities she had to help people at Riverview General Hospital. She thought, too, about the enormous sacrifices* Tala made on her behalf. "Without my mother," Gloria thought, "I could never have entered a profession that has given me so much personal satisfaction." She would never find this kind of fulfillment* on the Number 12 bus, on the Internet, or even on the Scottish Highlands. From that moment on, she promised herself that she would never again indulge in silly romantic fantasies. She didn't need them. It didn't get better than seeing Joshua Garrett go home from the hospital. Gloria felt very lucky to have the real, rewarding life that she had.

One evening, soon after Joshua was released, Gloria looked up from her paperwork at the nurse's station. She caught a glimpse of a tall, dark-haired man in green scrubs entering

Room 514. "That must be Mr. Rosen's anesthesiologist," thought Gloria. Mr. Rosen was preparing for a coronary artery bypass[+] in the morning, and the doctor was probably there for his pre-operative interview. She had heard some other nurses talking about the new anesthesiologist making the rounds. "He's *very* cute," commented Anh, nodding in his direction. "Have you met him?"

"No, I haven't," answered Gloria, her face, for some reason, turning a little red. Then Gloria looked down again at her paperwork and said matter-of-factly, "Anh, you need to collect these blood samples[+] and bring them to the lab right away. Also, Mr. Bowman in Room 511 just went down for some X-rays. While he's gone, please put clean linens on his bed."

"Okay, I can do that," said Anh, seeing that Gloria wasn't amused by her comment. Once Anh had disappeared with the blood samples, Gloria looked up again. For a moment, her eyes wandered over to the doorway of Room 514. She was a little curious, actually. After all, she had made a point of introducing herself to dozens of new doctors and nurses at the hospital over the years. This was just one more—"cute" or not. It was almost time to record Mr. Rosen's vital signs anyway. Gloria stood up, but as she did so she received a call from Mrs. Tweed in Room 521. First, she needed to respond to her.

After she had adjusted Mrs. Tweed's IV, Gloria headed into Room 514 to check on Mr. Rosen. His anesthesiologist had just left, but she checked his chart to see if there were any last-minute instructions for her to follow. "How did everything go with your pre-operative interview?" asked Gloria, while monitoring Mr. Rosen's blood pressure.

"Oh, very well," Mr. Rosen replied. "The anesthesiologist seemed like a nice kid. He promised me that I wouldn't feel a thing during my surgery."

"And you won't. I'm sure he is very capable," said Gloria, recording Mr. Rosen's vital signs on his chart.

"He seemed a little young, though, to be a doctor," said Mr. Rosen. "Of course, now that I'm seventy-eight, everybody looks young to me. To me, you look like a *baby*."

Gloria laughed out loud. "Every person on the surgical team at this hospital is board-certified[+], Mr. Rosen. Please rest assured that your doctor is very well-trained." Gloria had had this conversation with many patients over the years. Anticipating* surgery was often very stressful. Gloria reached over and put her hand over Mr. Rosen's. "Believe me. Your anesthesiologist has had a lot of experience—and years and years of study."

"If you say so," said Mr. Rosen. "I just hope that Dr. Castillo did all of his homework."

Chapter 13

A Terrible Disappointment

"Doctor *Castillo*?" said Gloria to herself, as she left Mr. Rosen's room. "Certainly not *that* Castillo. Impossible." The dreadful boy who once pointed and fired a ketchup bottle at her could not have possibly evolved into Mr. Rosen's anesthesiologist. Also, from where she sat behind the counter at the nurse's station, he appeared to be very handsome. "But it's a fairly common name," thought Gloria. "There could be a few Castillos working here at Riverview General Hospital. Besides, Mr. Rosen may have gotten his name wrong. It could have been Doctor *Casillas*, or Doctor *Costello*, or Doctor *Cisneros*." After all, patients frequently made mistakes with Gloria's name—even when she wore a name tag.

Gloria got off work at 6:00p.m. and was able to join her mother for dinner at home. "Delicious, Mom, as usual," said Gloria gratefully, as she swallowed her last bite of fried fish and rice.

"I'm glad you enjoyed it," replied Tala, wiping her mouth with her napkin. "I made the same thing for Mr. and Mrs. Campbell today, and they liked it, too."

"How's your reading going?" Gloria asked. "Does Mrs. Campbell like all of the excitement on the Highlands?"

"Well, we haven't read much of that one yet," answered Tala. "I've been a little too busy with other things: helping Mr. Campbell, cooking and cleaning."

"They're very lucky to have you, Mom," said Gloria, proudly. "You're a fantastic caregiver." Then she got up from the table, pushed in her chair, and began removing all the plates and silverware from the table. "I've got the dishes tonight, Mom. Please sit down and relax. You've had a busy day, too."

"If you insist," said Tala. "My legs are a little tired from standing." Still, she got up and followed her daughter into the kitchen.

"So," continued Gloria. "Tomorrow is Wednesday. Are you getting together with your friends for mahjong in the afternoon?"

"Yes, I hope so," answered Tala, scraping some leftover fish out of the frying pan and putting it into a plastic container. "But I do need to work from 6:00a.m. to noon for the Campbells again tomorrow. Wanda was supposed to be there, but she has a doctor's appointment in the morning. It's okay, though. She'll work the early shift for me on Friday."

"I think it's nice how you can all be so flexible," said Gloria, as she ran hot water into the dishpan and squirted in some detergent.

"Yes, we work it out," said Tala. "We just make sure someone is there with the Campbells all the time, especially with their family living so far away. They really can't be alone anymore. And Mr. Campbell requires more care than Mrs. Campbell can handle at her age. Anyway, I will manage to get to my mahjong game. We don't usually start until 2:00p.m. or so."

"Good, Mom. I'm glad you have that activity in your life. It's mentally stimulating—and you get to hear all the gossip swirling around the Filipino community."

"That's not why I go," laughed Tala. "But I will admit that I hear a good story now and then."

"Hey, Mom," said Gloria, rinsing off a dinner plate and putting it into the dish drainer. "I just thought of something.

"Do you remember a few weeks ago when you mentioned Riza Castillo's son, Antonio?"

"Yes," replied Tala quietly. "I remember."

"You said that Antonio worked at Riverview General Hospital, didn't you?"

"Apparently so," said Tala, pouring herself a glass of water. "Do you want to watch the news with me?"

"Maybe in a minute," said Gloria, turning away from the sink. "But about Antonio, do you remember *where* he worked in the hospital?"

"Oh, it doesn't matter, does it? You weren't interested in this information a few weeks ago. Why do you care now? It's almost time for the news," said Tala, obviously trying to change the subject.

"I'm just curious, Mom. That's all," said Gloria, gripping the pot scrubber tightly in her hand. Meanwhile, Tala had walked into the living room and turned on the TV. She waited a few moments before she replied.

"I think he's a doctor of some kind," said Tala, indifferently. "An anesthesiologist—or whatever. Who cares?" Gloria felt a strange sensation in her stomach. Then she walked out of the kitchen and into the living room with the wet pot scrubber still in her hand. Just as Tala had done a few weeks ago, Gloria now stood directly in front of the TV and faced her mother.

"*Who cares?* Well, I guess that I do, Mom. Did you forget that a month ago you and Riza were ready to arrange our marriage?"

"Never mind about that," said Tala. "Besides, your social life has gotten busier. You've been going out a little more, haven't you?"

"My social life is non-existent, Mom," said Gloria quite seriously. "But I'm okay with that. I was just wondering about Antonio. A *doctor?* That's quite surprising, really. I never would have predicted* that."

"Forget about Antonio, dear. I wish that I had never mentioned his name," said Tala, impatiently. "And you're dripping water on my nice carpet with that thing." Gloria held the wet pot scrubber more tightly so it wouldn't drip.

"Why do you say that, Mom? I'll admit that I was wrong to assume that Antonio was still that horrible kid. Believe me, I'm not chasing after him, but perhaps I'll say hello the next time I see him."

"Don't bother," sighed Tala, picking up the remote. Then she looked at her daughter sympathetically. "I really hate to tell you this, Gloria. But I suppose I should warn you: Antonio *doesn't want* to meet you."

Chapter 14

Hurt Feelings

Gloria left the room without another word and returned to the kitchen. She began to clean the rice pot furiously with the pot scrubber that she still held in her hand. "Antonio doesn't want to meet me," thought Gloria. "Ugh! That means that his mother suggested the idea and he flat-out refused." The strange sensation in her stomach began to feel almost painful. "Well," she thought, "I guess I flat-out refused, too. But Antonio didn't *know* that I had refused. Maybe he has seen me at the hospital and thinks I'm very unattractive. Or maybe he thinks that nurses aren't good enough for doctors. Or...I don't know what he thinks! But Mom is right, I suppose. *Who cares?*"

Gloria had recently made a promise to herself. She needed to stay completely focused on what was real and important in life: her patients at Riverview General Hospital—and her mother, of course. For some reason, however, this conversation with Tala had touched a nerve. Perhaps she was feeling especially vulnerable* after her pathetic attempts to enter the dating world. It was bad enough to be rejected by Antonio Castillo, who may have seen her once or twice on the fifth floor. But just before that, even Boomer, what's-his-name's dog, had rejected her. She had to admit that these were huge blows to her ego*. And, yes, it was totally embarrassing—because the fact was that she obviously *did* care. She cared a lot.

After Gloria finished the dishes, she returned to the living room but didn't sit down next to her mother on the sofa. "If you don't mind, Mom, I think I'm going to pass on watching TV tonight. I'd prefer to go to my room and read."

"I hope I didn't hurt your feelings," said Tala, looking up at Gloria and sensing instantly that she had. "I honestly didn't think this would bother you."

"It's okay, Mom," said Gloria, really trying to fight back the tears that she could feel forming in her eyes. "It doesn't matter. I think I'm just tired."

"Someday, you will meet the right person for you," added Tala, standing up and giving her daughter a warm hug. Unfortunately, her mother's hug didn't reassure her at all. It made her feel even worse.

"Or not," said Gloria. "But let's please not talk about this stuff ever again, okay? It just isn't helpful. Good night."

In her bedroom, Gloria didn't pick up her book. She didn't open her laptop to observe the exciting lives her friends were leading on their social-networking* websites. Instead, she threw herself onto her bed, buried her face into her pillow, and let the tears stream out of her eyes.

Chapter 15

Watch Out, Tala!

Tala left for work early the next morning, before the sun came up. She walked the familiar three blocks west and two blocks north and arrived at the Campbells' house a few minutes before 6:00a.m. As usual, Mrs. Campbell was already up, but needed Tala's help to get Mr. Campbell out of bed and ready for the day. Once Tala had positioned Mr. Campbell in his favorite chair in front of the TV, she wandered into the kitchen to cook breakfast. "Let's see," said Tala, peering into their refrigerator. "I think we'll have scrambled eggs, toast, orange juice, and coffee. How does that sound?" she asked Mr. and Mrs. Campbell, who were sitting contentedly behind their TV trays in the living room.

"Fine by me," answered Mrs. Campbell. "What do you think, Harry?" When Mr. Campbell didn't answer, Mrs. Campbell raised her voice, "HARRY, WHAT DO YOU THINK ABOUT TALA MAKING SCRAMBLED EGGS?"

"Okay," said Mr. Campbell. "Sounds good." So Tala went about her daily tasks: cooking and serving breakfast, washing dishes, administering medications at the right times, changing beds, washing, drying, and putting away two loads of laundry, vacuuming, assisting Mr. Campbell with his arm and leg exercises, and watering the plants.

Mrs. Campbell looked at the clock at 11:30. "Do you have time to read a bit before you leave?" she asked. Tala knew that Sophia would be arriving in thirty minutes to prepare their lunches. "Maybe just one chapter?" she

51

continued, picking up *Passion on the Highlands* and offering it to Tala. "You know that I don't see as well as I used to. And I love to hear you read." So Tala pulled up a chair next to Mrs. Campbell and opened the book to Chapter 4. It was an exciting part, indeed. Colin had his first glimpse of Abbie running around the Highlands with her friends: "*Colin observed her beautiful red hair, pretty face, and slim figure. He heard her happy laugh that trilled like a songbird. Colin couldn't breathe. He felt his heart pounding in his chest…*"

"Just the way I felt when I first saw you," interrupted Mr. Campbell, surprising both Mrs. Campbell and Tala because they thought he never listened to—or heard—these stories.

"It's the way you *still* feel, Harry," said Mrs. Campbell, prompting a riot of laughter from all three of them. Just then Sophia came through the front door.

"To be continued," said Tala, wiping the tears of laughter from her eyes. "I'll read more tomorrow afternoon, okay?" She exchanged information with Sophia and waved to the Campbells as she walked out the front door.

Tala looked down at the sidewalk as she reflected on *Passion on the Highlands*. She knew that these romance novels were meant to be entertaining, but she couldn't help but also feel a little sad when she thought about her own life. Once she, too, had been deeply in love with Hilario, Gloria's father. "It was a wonderful feeling," thought Tala, walking toward Main Street. "Of course, people miss it when, for whatever reason, it goes away."

Remembering her life with Hilario could still bring tears to her eyes. She had been desperately lonely for years. She knew her daughter had suffered greatly from losing her father at such a young age. And now, here was Gloria, at the prime* of her life, but unwilling or unable to find someone to share her life with. Yes, Tala was glad to have Gloria's company and support, but it just didn't feel fair to her daughter.

Tala remembered their awkward conversation the night before. Gloria had clearly been upset by it. Tala had even heard her crying quietly in her bedroom. The sound broke her heart, but she respected her daughter's privacy and did not offer to console* her. She understood Gloria very well, and knew when she wished to be left alone. "Of course, she needs someone in her life. Poor girl," thought Tala as she stepped off of the curb, her eyes focusing on the black asphalt below her. After taking several steps into the intersection, Tala heard a terrible screeching sound. The last thing she remembered was looking up and seeing a car heading straight for her.

Chapter 16

Critical Condition

The driver of the car was unable to stop before striking the woman who was crossing the street. The impact tossed Tala up into the air and then down onto the hard, black asphalt. She lay motionless on the road as other drivers and pedestrians* quickly stopped. Soon, a large crowd had gathered at the scene. "Oh, no!" screamed the driver, a young woman, who had hit her. "The light was green! Where did she come from? I didn't…I didn't…see her!"

"I've already called 911!" said one man.

"She's unconscious⁺," said another woman, who had raced over to Tala to help. "But she doesn't need CPR because she has a pulse⁺…and she appears to be breathing." Then the woman knelt down next to Tala and covered her with her coat.

Within minutes both the paramedics⁺ and the police arrived. Tala groaned softly as a team of paramedics quickly attended to her. When the paramedics determined that Tala wasn't breathing effectively, they hastily* gave her oxygen. Then they moved her onto a stretcher and into the ambulance⁺. With sirens blaring, they sped off in the direction of Riverview General Hospital. However, the police remained at the accident scene for a long time. They gathered statements* from several witnesses as well as from the distressed driver. Everyone agreed that, for some reason, the victim had ignored the red light and walked directly in front of the oncoming traffic.

Tala was taken to the trauma center at Riverview General Hospital. From the identification and information that she carried in her purse, the hospital staff learned who she was. They also learned about her blood type and allergies, and who they needed to contact in case of an emergency. Their immediate efforts, however, were to stabilize* Tala and identify her life-threatening injuries. Because she was fortunate to be in a hospital with an excellent trauma center, she had the advantage of a large team of doctors and nurses who could perform a variety of diagnostic tests[+] and assess her condition quickly. Tala's trauma team consisted of several doctors: a general surgeon, an orthopedic[+] surgeon, a neurosurgeon[+], an emergency doctor, a radiologist[+], and an anesthesiologist. They worked swiftly to manage her breathing, conduct tests, and perform other medical procedures. There were also three nurses who monitored her vital signs, began an IV, and obtained blood samples. Everyone knew that a patient's chance of survival was much better if he or she received help within one hour of a serious injury. This was called the *golden hour,* and they had to work fast. As Tala was found to have multiple fractures[+], lacerations[+], and internal injuries, she was wheeled into surgery almost immediately.

Meanwhile, Eliza Green, the RN who had Tala's emergency contact information, needed to call *Gloria Navarro,* a person who she assumed was the patient's daughter. Notifying a relative of an accident was always a difficult phone call to make, and this one was especially hard because of the patient's critical[+] condition. Eliza picked up the white card from Tala's wallet and looked at the three telephone numbers listed for Gloria Navarro: cell, home, and work. No one answered at either the cell or home number, but she left two brief messages anyway. Then she looked closely at the work number. "Oh, my gosh!" Eliza said to one of the other nurses on staff. "Look at this telephone number. Her next of kin[+] apparently works somewhere here at Riverview General Hospital." Then she dialed the number and got the hospital operator.

"Riverview General Hospital. How may I direct your call?"

"This is Eliza Green in the trauma center. I need to find a Gloria Navarro, N-A-V-A-R-R-O, who works somewhere in the hospital. Can you please connect me to her extension right away? This is an emergency."

Chapter 17

Waiting

When Laura found Gloria in a patient's room on the fifth floor, she informed her that there was an emergency telephone call for her at the nurse's station. Gloria hurried over to the phone, wondering what kind of hospital emergency it could be. When Eliza Green from the trauma center identified herself, Gloria still assumed that this was a professional call and not a personal one. But when she heard the name *Tala Navarro*, she gasped loudly and sank into a chair. Her mother had been in an accident and was, at this moment, in the trauma center on the first floor of Riverview General Hospital. As Gloria knew very well, Eliza couldn't release any more details. She had to come down in person for a full explanation of her mother's condition.

Gloria began to shake and her legs felt weak. Laura and two other nurses looked at her with concern as she hung up the phone, turning around to reveal an anguished* expression. "Oh, my gosh! What's wrong?" asked Laura.

"It's my mother," said Gloria. "There's been some kind of accident. She's here—in the trauma center. I've…I've got to get down there!"

"Of course," said Agnes, the nursing director on the fifth floor, who rushed up immediately to assist her. "We have plenty of staff right now. I'll call in someone else if we need to. Please go. Right now," she said putting her arm around Gloria gently. "Would you like me to go with you, dear?"

"No, thanks, Agnes," Gloria said, "I can do it." Gloria tried to compose herself. In a moment, she regained the strength in her legs and walked as fast as she could toward the elevator.

When Gloria arrived on the first floor of the trauma center, she approached the nurse's station. "Excuse me," she said, in a high-pitched voice that she could barely recognize as her own. "I just received a telephone call. I'm Tala Navarro's daughter, Gloria."

"Oh, come right this way, Ms. Navarro," said a nurse at the station. "I called you. My name is Eliza Green."

Gloria followed Eliza through a side door and into a private area.

"Please...please tell me what's happened," begged Gloria once Eliza had offered her a chair. "Can I please see my mother?"

"Your mother was hit by a car this afternoon while crossing a street," said Eliza. "She has multiple fractures, lacerations, and internal injuries. She's in an extremely critical condition. Right now, she's in surgery. We will update you on her condition just as soon as we can." Gloria put her face into her hands.

"Oh, no!" she said. "Oh, Mom, no!" Eliza handed Gloria a box of tissues as tears were now flowing down her cheeks.

"Please know that we're doing everything we can for your mother. She's in very good hands and has an excellent medical team monitoring her every second." Eliza's comforting words sounded very familiar to Gloria. She had also spoken them many times to countless patients whose families were distraught about their loved ones. It felt horrible to be on this side of the conversation, with someone patting her hand and bringing her a glass of water. "This can't be happening," thought Gloria. She thought about the last time she'd seen her mother and what she'd said to her last night: *"Let's please not talk about this stuff ever again, okay?"* How childishly she'd behaved. And how ridiculous it seemed now. What if she couldn't talk to her mother—about anything—ever again?

Tala was in surgery for nearly four more hours. During that time, Gloria sat, stood, or paced nervously around the waiting area. Although it was now clear that Gloria was an RN at this hospital, the trauma center nurses discouraged her from trying to see her mother. They urged her to wait for someone on the surgical team to come out and speak to her first.

Finally, after what seemed like an eternity*, a young doctor in surgical scrubs came out of the double doors leading into the waiting area. "Ms. Navarro?" he asked. "I'm Dr. Castillo, your mother's anesthesiologist."

Gloria stood up from her chair and walked slowly toward Antonio. She looked into his eyes and pressed her hands together. After hours of agony*, she was now terrified to hear what he had to say. "Oh, please," she said, with a sob escaping from her throat. "Please tell me that my mother is still alive."

Chapter 18

Relief

"Your mother is alive," said Antonio kindly. "And she is stable. She made it through surgery without any complications." Gloria listened intently—and continued to wipe her tears—as Antonio described the procedures that Tala had had in the operating room. The surgeon had to stabilize the complex fractures in her left leg and stop the internal bleeding. The accident left her with serious breaks in her femur, patella, tibia, and fibula[+]. "I'm afraid she's in for a long recovery. We'll need to monitor her closely in the hospital for a while. Then there will be bed rest and many weeks of rehabilitation[+]. And she'll definitely need assistance at home."

"That isn't a problem," said Gloria. "I live with her. And I'll make arrangements for people to be there when I'm at work."

"She has a lot of metal in her left leg—plates and screws," said Antonio. "But she'll eventually walk again. She's very lucky, really. No spinal cord injury. No neurological[+] damage. Her vital organs are working well. She appears to be a very healthy woman, overall. She should recover fully from this accident."

Just when Gloria thought she had shed her last tear, new tears—ones of joy and relief—sprang out of her eyes.

"Thank you so much, Dr. Castillo. Really, this is wonderful news. I was so worried that I'd lost her." Sometime during this conversation, Antonio had recognized Gloria as the young woman he had seen in the hospital cafeteria a few weeks ago. Although her face was red and swollen from crying, and she continued to wipe her eyes and nose with tissues, Antonio still had the same feeling that he had seen her before.

"You know," said Antonio, "you look very familiar. Even your name sounds familiar. Please don't take this the wrong way, but *don't I know you from someplace?*"

"I think you might," laughed Gloria, wadding up a bunch of wet tissues and dropping them into the trash. "Is your first name, by any chance, *Antonio?*"

"Yes, it is," answered Antonio. "How did you know?"

"Thank you so much, Dr. Castillo. I was so worried that I'd lost her."

"Your mother, Riza, and my mother, Tala, are old friends. My mom told me that you worked here a few weeks ago."

"And come to think of it," Antonio said, remembering the annoying telephone call from his mother, "my mother told me the same thing about *you*." Antonio smiled broadly, took Gloria's hand in his, and shook it warmly.

"Well, Gloria. I know this isn't the ideal way to meet someone, but I'm *very* glad to meet you."

After a few minutes, Gloria was given permission to see her mother in the recovery room. Antonio accompanied her toward the area where Tala was regaining consciousness. On the way, Antonio introduced Gloria to Dr. Claire Matthews, the orthopedic surgeon who had operated on her mother.

"I already know her," said Dr. Matthews. "We've met many times on the fifth floor. She's a wonderful nurse and a dear person. Gloria, I'm so sorry about your mother's accident."

"Thank you so much for putting my mother back together again," said Gloria, hugging her appreciatively. "I certainly didn't expect her to end up in the trauma center today."

"She'll be okay," Dr. Matthews said. "I'm warning you, though. You may not recognize her when you see her. Your mom has been through a very rough day—and nearly five hours of surgery. But I'm sure she'll be glad to know you're here."

Antonio led the way into a smaller room where Tala lay on a bed. But Gloria did recognize her, in spite of the oxygen, the IV lines, the cuts and bruises, and her left leg elevated above her bed. She wanted so much to embrace her mother, but just stroked her shoulder gently instead.

"Hey, Mom," Gloria said quietly. Her mother opened her eyes and focused them on her daughter. "Don't worry.

You're okay. The doctors said you're going to be fine." Tala closed her eyes again and nodded her head slightly.

"Hi, Mrs. Navarro," Antonio added. "I'm Riza's son, Antonio—and your anesthesiologist. Your surgery went beautifully." Tala opened her eyes for a moment and both Gloria and Antonio saw the faintest smile inside the clear oxygen mask. "Unfortunately, I doubt that your daughter has eaten anything all day," added Antonio, winking across the bed at Gloria. "Would it be okay if I took her to the cafeteria for a bowl of soup?" Tala closed her eyes again, but gave Antonio a thumbs-up sign.

Chapter 19

A Lunch Shared

Antonio held the door open for Gloria and then brought her over to an empty table. "I want you to sit down here and tell me what you want. I'll bring it to you."

"Oh you don't have to do that," argued Gloria. "After all, you've been in surgery all afternoon."

"Yes, but my mother didn't get hit by a car."

"Okay." Gloria laughed, for the first time in several hours. "You win. I would love a bowl of chicken noodle soup."

In a few minutes, Antonio came back to the table with the chicken soup—and a salad, a glass of milk, and a piece of chocolate cake. "That's to keep up your strength," said Antonio. "Besides, the cake is pretty good here."

"I really appreciate this," said Gloria, smiling at him. "I am starving, actually." Then Antonio brought over another tray with a hamburger, a glass of lemonade, and some fruit.

"You know," said Antonio, as he sat down across the table from her, "I think I saw you here in the cafeteria once before."

"Really?" asked Gloria, taking a bite of her salad. "When?"

"A few weeks ago," replied Antonio. "You were sitting over there—along the wall. I was tempted to say hello, but you were totally engrossed in a book." Gloria's face turned a little red as she remembered that it was probably *Passion on the Highlands*. "And it must have been a good one because you didn't look up for a moment—even when I asked you for the ketchup," Antonio added, picking up the plastic bottle of ketchup off of

64

the table. At this point, Gloria burst out laughing. "What?" said Antonio. "Did I say something funny?"

"Please, don't," said Gloria.

"Please don't what?" asked Antonio. "I'm totally confused."

"Please don't...squirt that at me," said Gloria, laughing, "like you did twenty years ago at the picnic on the lake." At that point, Antonio slapped the top of the table and exclaimed, "I totally remember that! Was that little girl...*you*?" When Gloria nodded, he threw back his head and had a huge laugh. "Well, I thought you looked familiar when I saw you here before." Then he jokingly* aimed the ketchup bottle at Gloria.

"Don't even think about it," said Gloria. "Besides, that's not a good look on a nurse. I'll frighten all of my patients."

"I suppose you're right," said Antonio, still laughing. "But that's just what some boys do when they like someone."

After they finished eating, Gloria had a lot to do. She checked in on her mother, who was resting comfortably. She went back to the nurse's station on the fifth floor and told her co-workers more about the accident and Tala's condition. "I'm off, though, for the next two days," said Gloria, "so I can spend time at the hospital with her."

"Gloria, dear, if you need to rearrange your schedule here and there, just let me know," said Agnes. "Of course you need to be there for your mother."

It was nearly 10:00p.m. when Gloria finally arrived home. She felt sad to walk in the front door and find no one there. She was used to her mother's warm greeting and offering of food. "What an incredible mother I have," thought Gloria, fighting the urge to cry again. "And thank goodness that I have her still."

Gloria wandered into the kitchen and opened a drawer. She reached in and took out her mother's old address book with the daisies on the cover. Then she grabbed another handful of tissues because it wouldn't be easy to make these phone calls. However, she absolutely needed to let Mr. and Mrs. Campbell know—and all of their caregivers. They certainly couldn't depend on Tala's help for a while. She needed to contact Eva and her mother's other mahjong friends. She had to call her uncle in the Philippines, who would spread the word around the extended family. This was difficult news to deliver, but many, many people loved Tala and had a right to know what had happened to her. Besides, Gloria really couldn't handle this situation alone. She needed their support almost as much as her mother did.

Chapter 20

New Love

Tala stayed at Riverview General Hospital for over two weeks. Then she went to a rehabilitation hospital, located in an adjoining building, for another two weeks. For an active and independent person like Tala, recovering from this injury was very frustrating. She was used to helping other people and not depending on them for help. She was unhappy about spending so much time in bed. She disliked taking her medications. Since Tala had always been in very good health, dealing with a lot of pain was hard for her—physically and mentally. However, the experience was bearable because of the kindness and encouragement that she received from doctors, nurses, physical therapists and, of course, her daughter Gloria.

Gloria managed to check on Tala frequently while she was in the hospital. Also, as the news of Tala's accident spread, it resulted in a steady stream of visitors: mahjong friends, church friends, and neighborhood friends. One day, Mrs. Campbell asked Dora to drive her to the rehabilitation hospital while Wanda stayed at home with Mr. Campbell. Mrs. Campbell brought Tala a big bouquet of flowers. Then she pulled *Passion on the Highlands* out of her purse and jokingly insisted that Tala read it to her. "Go ahead, Tala," Mrs. Campbell said, winking at Dora. "It's only your leg that's broken. You can still *read* to me." This comment gave Tala one of her first big laughs since the accident. "I miss your company, Tala," continued Mrs. Campbell. "I can't wait until you're well enough to come home."

"I can't either," said Tala. "I'm standing and taking more steps every day. I am taking my rehabilitation exercises very seriously."

"Good," said Mrs. Campbell. "Tomorrow, I'm sending Mr. Campbell over here to help you exercise." This comment sent all three of them into fits of laughter.

One other regular visitor was Antonio Castillo. He often stopped by to see how Tala was doing. In the weeks since her accident, he had also shared many meals with Gloria—both inside the hospital cafeteria and away from it. Antonio and Gloria thoroughly enjoyed each other's company, much to the delight of their mothers. It made Tala determined to get well and back to her kitchen to cook for both Gloria *and* Antonio. And it rather annoyed her that Riza had that opportunity now.

One Monday evening, Gloria and Antonio visited Tala together in her room. Gloria shared the details of her dinner at Antonio's parents' house the evening before. "Mrs. Castillo had it all: *pancit, lumpia,* sticky rice, and every other Filipino food you can imagine." But when Antonio noticed Tala looking a little sad, he interrupted Gloria.

"Yes, my mother is a *pretty* good cook. But she isn't a great one, like you, Mrs. Navarro. Gloria tells me that you're just incredible in the kitchen." After this comment, a big smile spread across Tala's face.

"Right!" said Gloria, "No one can top your cooking, Mom." Then she looked over at Antonio appreciatively. In addition to being a very handsome and caring doctor, he was also a very thoughtful person, who knew just what her mother needed to hear.

At the end of visiting hours, Gloria and Antonio left Tala's room. Antonio insisted on taking Gloria home—something he was in the habit of doing often. Gloria slipped her hand into his while they walked through the parking structure toward Antonio's car. "Just so you know," said Gloria, "I am a terrible cook and I hate spending hours in the kitchen."

"Is that so?" asked Antonio, pretending to be surprised. "Why didn't you tell me this before we started dating?" Gloria laughed out loud. "So, I need to understand something if we decide to move forward in this relationship," said Antonio matter-of-factly, trying to hide his smile. "If I want to eat a decent, home-cooked meal, I'm going to have to stay on *very* good terms with your mother."

"That is correct," said Gloria, squeezing his hand. "Everything I make needs to be covered in a lot of ketchup."

"That's fine with me," said Antonio, leaning toward Gloria and giving her a kiss on the cheek. "Ketchup happens to be one of my favorite foods."

Chapter 21

Tala Comes Home

Finally, almost five weeks after her accident, Tala was given permission to return home. She clapped her hands with joy as Gloria wheeled her through the front door. Tala was finally back in her very own home and the sight of the familiar surroundings brought tears to her eyes. "My sofa! My dining room table!" she exclaimed. "My very own bed! You don't know how happy I am to see them again." Of course, Tala still wore a long boot-type cast⁺. And she needed to use either a wheelchair or a walker to get from place to place. But her leg was healing and she felt grateful to be alive after such a horrible accident.

Naturally, Gloria assisted her at home when she could, but they had to rely on some outside help. Tala's good friends and co-workers, Sophia, Wanda, and Dora, all volunteered to work for a few hours a week until Tala could take care of herself independently. They assisted Tala with bathing and dressing. They took her to the numerous doctor and physical therapy appointments. Also, many meals were delivered for both Tala and Gloria from among her large circle of mahjong friends. And, when Tala felt up to it, the Wednesday games that were previously held at the community center were relocated to her living room. It was really good for Tala to focus on other things besides her pain and temporary disability⁺.

Tala was deeply touched* by the outpouring of love and attention that she received from her co-workers and friends. For years after Hilario died, Tala often wondered if staying in the U.S. had been the right decision. Most of her extended family still lived in the Philippines, so she definitely would have had more emotional support there. Nonetheless, Tala firmly believed that the U.S. offered Gloria more educational and professional opportunities. Therefore, she chose not to return to her native country. And now, it was clear that Tala also had an amazing support system in her adopted country. In addition to her daughter, it was obvious that many other people in her community cared deeply about her.

Another pleasure in Tala's life was to observe her daughter coming home from work—sometimes with Antonio. A couple of evenings a week, they entered the house with grocery bags and strict instructions from Antonio: "You're not lifting a finger," he said kindly as he wheeled Tala into the kitchen. "But can you please give us step-by-step instructions so we can actually eat this stuff?" Tala loved feeling useful and issued advice with great enthusiasm. "Antonio, please turn up the heat a little higher on the right-front burner. Gloria, that celery needs to be chopped a bit smaller. Antonio, you must sauté those vegetables for a while longer. Gloria, that sauce will taste better if you add a little more garlic. Yes, that's it."

It was also very satisfying for Tala to see the big change in her daughter. The exhausted young woman who used to throw herself onto the sofa after work seemed completely transformed. Now, even after a long shift at the hospital, Gloria was laughing and full of energy, especially when Antonio was around. After a delicious dinner that Tala jokingly described as "not bad for beginners," Gloria leapt up from the table. She and Antonio laughed and talked as they put away the leftover food and washed the dishes. Her newfound happiness was contagious*. It made Tala very happy, too.

One evening after Antonio had left, Gloria helped her mother get ready for bed. Tala couldn't help teasing her daughter a little as Gloria gently helped her onto the bed, placing the injured leg into a comfortable position. "Well, as you can finally see, Antonio isn't such a horrible person after all," said Tala.

"Yes," Gloria replied, positioning a pillow carefully under Tala's leg. "I will admit that I was completely wrong about that."

"So I suppose that Riza Castillo and I were quite *right* in wanting the two of you to meet for coffee sometime."

"Apparently so, Mom," said Gloria, trying very hard not to laugh.

"But since you didn't agree to that," continued Tala, mischievously*, "I had to get *hit by a car* in order for it to happen." Gloria smiled and then looked her mother squarely in the eyes.

"I will never doubt your wisdom again, Mom. And I am so happy that Antonio Castillo is in my life. And I want you, also, in my life for many more years. So *please*, promise me that you'll always look both ways before you cross the street."

"I think I can promise that," said Tala, kissing her daughter's forehead. "Good night."

Chapter 22

Back to Work

It was nearly six months before Tala was able to resume working for Mr. and Mrs. Campbell. Although she was now able to walk a fair distance, she still limped slightly and relied on a cane for stability.

"You can go back to work, but please don't overdo it," warned Dr. Matthews, who had examined Tala many times during the past weeks and months. "Don't do any heavy lifting or anything else that could cause you to lose your balance and fall."

Meanwhile, Mr. and Mrs. Campbell, Sophia, Wanda, and Dora had all agreed to make some scheduling changes. For now, they allowed Tala to work only the afternoon shifts. Then she did not have to handle the more physical aspects of the job: helping Mr. Campbell in and out of bed, in and out of the shower, and in and out of his chair. "We don't want to lose you again," said Mr. Campbell. "Just give me my medicine and make sure that the house doesn't burn down."

"Yes," Mrs. Campbell added. "And, well, read to *me*, of course."

It felt very strange for Tala to be walking to work again after so much time had passed. In her mind, it had felt like a hundred years since the accident. She reflected on those miserable weeks in the hospital, staring at the ceiling. She thought about the months of inactivity at home, annoyingly confined to a wheelchair or completely dependent on the walker. How happy she was to be out in the world again.

Tala walked toward the intersection where the accident had occurred. As she approached it, she began to feel uneasy. She still had a terrifying memory of the screeching sound and the sight of a car heading straight for her. The next thing she remembered was waking up in a hospital room with her leg elevated above the bed. Tala anxiously pushed the button at the crosswalk, but ignored the first three green traffic lights. Even though the Walk sign flashed persistently, Tala stayed perfectly still on the sidewalk. "People drive too fast on this street," thought Tala to herself. "I *can't* walk quickly. What if I don't make it to the other side before the light turns red?" Finally, on the fourth green light, Tala summoned the courage to look both ways. Then she put one foot down on the street and then the other. In a few seconds, she had safely crossed it.

Naturally, Mr. Campbell, Mrs. Campbell and Dora were all delighted to see Tala walk through the front door for the afternoon shift. Tala greeted them all with warm hugs. Mrs. Campbell refused to allow Tala to do any cooking or housework that day. Dora had already set up a TV tray for her next to the other two. Then she proceeded to bring her a sandwich and some iced tea. "And we know you like apple pie, Tala," added Dora as she put on her sweater and fumbled in her purse for the car keys. "So there's a nice dessert for all of you to eat this afternoon."

"Thank you," said Tala, appreciatively. "But I have to do *something* or I cannot, in good conscience, earn money."

"Just finish that awful book," laughed Dora. "Because we are through with *Passion on the Highlands*, *Passion on the Lowlands*, or *Passion in Any Other Land*! Well, um, of course we love the updates about your daughter and the handsome doctor. But Wanda, Sophia, and I will gladly leave the task of romantic fiction completely to you."

"It's a deal," laughed Tala.

"Now eat up," said Mrs. Campbell with a twinkle in her eye. "I've been waiting a long time to hear what's going to happen with Colin and Abbie. But perhaps you should start at the beginning again," she said, removing the bookmark before handing the paperback to Tala. "My memory isn't what it used to be, and I could use a little review."

"Very well," said Tala, taking a sip of her iced tea. "Back to the beginning, it is. Okay," she said, clearing her throat. "Chapter One. *Abbie ran to the top of the hill and spun around playfully in her bright green dress…*"

"You know," interrupted Mr. Campbell. "All these books are the same. And I can already tell you how it's going to end."

"My dear," responded Mrs. Campbell, "please don't deny me the pleasure of hearing our precious Tala's voice again. Here she is, alive and well, sitting in our living room. For me, that's the best part of the story."

Chapter 23

A Funny Misunderstanding

Gloria and Antonio had been dating for nearly a year when they got engaged. They were entirely committed to each other and felt quite sure that getting married was the right decision. Gloria had never met a kinder person than Antonio. Her attachment to him grew stronger every day. She had the highest regard for Antonio both as a person and as a doctor. Antonio claimed that, for him, it was *love at first sight*. And, according to Antonio, that first sight was neither in the cafeteria nor in the trauma unit of Riverview General Hospital. It was twenty years before that. He maintained* that the ketchup incident at the lake was the natural expression of an eleven-year-old boy's romantic feelings. "My sweet Gloria," said Antonio, with his hand over his heart. "What else was I to do?"

There were several things that Gloria and Antonio had in common. They were raised with the same beliefs and customs. They grew up eating a lot of the same foods. Their mothers were old friends, and they knew many of the same people in their community. However, their shared dedication to their jobs brought them even closer together. No one was more understanding than Gloria when Antonio suddenly had to leave a family function* in order to respond to a medical emergency. And no one was more understanding than Antonio when Gloria's countless tasks at the hospital required her to work overtime. Occasionally, when he was on the fifth floor, he would catch a glimpse of her assisting a patient or a doctor, and feel a tremendous sense of pride. He had never heard anyone at Riverview General Hospital speak of Gloria Navarro, the RN, without the greatest respect and admiration.

The announcement of their engagement brought ecstatic cheers from each of their mothers. Riza said that her son was the luckiest man in the world to marry such a lovely, accomplished young woman. And Tala declared that she would have happily broken twenty legs if she thought the outcome* would create this much happiness for everyone involved.

Gradually, the news of their engagement also leaked out among their friends and co-workers at Riverview General Hospital. People were unanimously* supportive; they couldn't imagine two people who deserved each other more. Antonio and Gloria rarely saw each other at work, but when they did, they conducted themselves very professionally. No patients or medical staff members would have ever guessed that they planned to be married in the future.

Shortly before their wedding, Mrs. Greenstein returned to Riverview General Hospital. Her first hip-replacement surgery had been very successful, and she was now admitted to the hospital for surgery on the other side. "Half of me feels like a young woman," she said to Gloria, shortly after she was brought up to the fifth floor, "but the other half still feels like an old one. It's time to feel young on both sides, don't you think?"

"I wholeheartedly agree," said Gloria, recording her temperature and blood pressure. "It's a pleasure to have you back with us, Mrs. Greenstein."

"Oh, I remember you all very well. And how was your wedding, dear? Was it like a fairy tale?"

"My wedding?" Gloria looked confused, and then her memory flashed to the very awkward conversation she had with Mrs. Greenstein more than a year ago. Gloria couldn't believe that a patient on pain medication had actually remembered it. Her face began to turn a little pink. "Oh, right. *That* wedding. Well, we had to postpone it for a while. But we've set the date for about three months from now." At that moment, there was a knock at the door.

"May I come in?" asked Antonio, standing in the doorway.

"Oh, yes!" replied Mrs. Greenstein, happily.

"Hello, Mrs. Greenstein. I'm Dr. Castillo," said Antonio, shaking her hand warmly. I'm here for your pre-operative interview. We've met before, haven't we?"

"Indeed, we have, Dr. Castillo! Dr. *Antonio* Castillo, isn't it? How nice to see you again. Yes, here I am for another new hip. The first one worked out beautifully. Now I'd like a matching one, please."

"That's the plan at 9:00a.m. tomorrow," said Dr. Castillo, taking a seat next to her bed. "So, let's discuss the anesthesia process."

"Well, I'll be on my way," said Gloria, quietly. "Please don't hesitate to call the nurse's station if you need anything, Mrs. Greenstein."

"Thank you, dear. Wonderful to see you again. And good luck with the wedding to *your* Antonio Castillo—not this doctor with the same name, who I mistook him for last year. Do you remember that silly conversation, Dr. Castillo? I thought *you* were the man that Gloria intended to marry." Now Gloria's face had gone from pink to bright red.

"Really?" asked Antonio, a large grin spreading across his face. "You know, I do seem to remember our conversation now."

"Well," interjected Gloria, "you see, Mrs. Greenstein, that other Antonio Castillo is no longer in the picture. He turned out to be a reckless young man who had terrible table manners and was simply unable to keep ketchup on a hamburger—where it belongs. Now I have accepted a proposal from *this* greatly improved Antonio Castillo," she said, pointing proudly in the direction of her anesthesiologist. "How's that for a happy ending?" Mrs. Greenstein looked delighted.

"Well, this is fabulous news, indeed!" exclaimed Mrs. Greenstein, looking at Gloria and Antonio approvingly. "I just knew you two were meant for each other. Now," she sighed, "if only my grandson, Larry, could find someone."

Chapter 24

Medical Match

Gloria and Antonio invited all of their family and friends to their wedding. Several people on both sides of their families came all the way from the Philippines to attend. All of Antonio's sisters and their families were there, of course. Many co-workers from Riverview General Hospital came to celebrate with them: Laura, Anh, Agnes, Dr. Matthews, and Dr. Nguyen, to name a few. Tala's entire mahjong circle was there. Mr. and Mrs. Campbell attended, accompanied by Sophia, Wanda, and Dora. Fortunately, Tala and Riza had many friends in common, and it seemed that they all came to celebrate with both the Navarros and the Castillos.

The ceremony had many traditional elements to it. First, it was in December, the most popular month for Filipino weddings. Gloria wore a lovely, long white dress. Antonio wore a white *Barong Tagalog*, a translucent* white embroidered shirt, and black pants. Both Riza and Danilo walked Antonio proudly up the aisle. Then Tala escorted Gloria up the aisle. It was with great happiness that she managed this without her cane, and all of the onlookers shared in her joy during this heartwarming moment.

The one-hour Mass included several Filipino wedding rituals*. There was the exchange of rings and the giving of the *arrhae*, the groom's gift to the bride of thirteen gold coins to symbolize his support. There was the lighting of wedding candles. There was the pinning of a veil over the bride and groom, signifying the clothing of two individuals who were now one. And there was the placing of their

It was with great happiness that Tala managed to escort Gloria up the aisle without her cane.

decorative *yugal*, a figure-eight shaped cord draped over Gloria and Antonio's necks and shoulders, representing the bond of marriage and fidelity.

Gloria and Antonio's reception* in the church hall offered an impressive selection of Filipino foods: *lumpia*, *pancit bihon*, *apritada*, *bola bola*, chicken *adobo*, *embutido*, and curried milkfish. But there were also some token American ones: hot dogs, hamburgers, and French fries served within reach of an enormous bottle of ketchup. "It just wouldn't be our wedding without it," insisted Antonio.

"Okay," agreed Gloria, smiling, "but I must warn you: if ketchup *accidentally* gets on my wedding dress, someone is going to end up at Riverview General Hospital."

There was also an incredible, four-tiered chocolate cake that Gloria jokingly described as "almost as good as the one you bought me in the hospital cafeteria."

There were many happy toasts to the new couple. The bride and groom spent hours greeting their guests and dancing. Shortly before their reception officially ended, Gloria and Antonio found Tala still sitting at a table among a cluster of her relatives. Tala already knew that, for now, Gloria had decided to move into Antonio's apartment. For one thing, it was nearer to the hospital and definitely more convenient for them. Weeks ago, Tala had assured them that she would be fine, and that this was definitely the thing to do. Besides, Tala would need the spare room, with her uncle and aunt from the Philippines staying with her for the next two months. "So," said Tala, blinking back tears at the sight of them getting ready to leave. "You are married now. I can't believe it. But I hope that I will continue to see you a lot."

"Of course you will," said Antonio. "We promise to visit often."

"Yes, Mom," added Gloria. "Hunger will bring my dear husband to your dining room table at least twice a week."

"I will look forward to that," sniffed Tala. Then she took both her daughter and her new son-in-law into her arms. "I am so happy for the two of you."

"Mom," said Gloria, a lump in her throat brought on by her mother's tears. "I will be grateful to you forever. You will always be in our lives and you will always have our support. That will never change."

"I'm glad to hear that," answered Tala.

"Yes," continued Antonio, with his arm around Tala's shoulder. "I have the best mother-in-law in the world. And I'm not just saying that because Gloria and I can't cook."

"I know that," said Tala, wiping her eyes. "Now, you need to get out of here and go on your honeymoon. You're not getting any younger, you know," she said with a sparkle in her eye. She then added, "I don't know whether or not I've ever mentioned this, Gloria, but…when I was your age, I was married *and had you!*"

"Well," said Antonio, "let's listen to your mother. I think that's the signal to start our honeymoon." They all laughed and hugged each other again.

"Thanks for everything, Mom," said Gloria. "You're the best." Then Gloria and Antonio turned away and walked toward the door.

EXERCISES

A Comprehension

Chapters 1 – 6 Write short answers to the following questions.

1 Why was Gloria not interested in meeting Antonio Castillo?

2 What ways did Gloria think of to meet men?

3 Why did Gloria lie to Mrs. Greenstein about having a fiancé?

4 Why was Tala nervous about calling her friend Riza?

5 Why was Antonio not interested in meeting Gloria?

6 Why was Tala so keen for Gloria to meet somebody?

Chapters 7 – 12 What do the underlined words in these sentences refer to?

7 "Surprisingly enough, she couldn't put <u>it</u> down."

8 "<u>It</u> was, perhaps, an old-fashioned view, but that's the way she saw it."

9 "He couldn't imagine letting <u>it</u> go just so he could go out more often."

10 "Gloria really didn't like the way <u>that</u> sounded and so after a few email messages, *she* eliminated *him*."

11 "At <u>that</u> moment, Gloria decided to stop trying to be spontaneous."

12 "She would never find <u>this kind of fulfillment</u> on the Number 12 bus, on the Internet, or even on the Scottish Highlands."

Chapters 13 – 18 Who said these words and to whom? Who or what were they talking about?

13 "I'm glad you have that activity in your life."

14 "Let's please not talk about this stuff ever again, okay?"

15 "Just the way I felt when I first saw you."

16 "Can you please connect me to her extension right away? This is an emergency."

17 "She's here—in the trauma center. I've…I've got to get down there!"

18 "And come to think of it, my mother told me the same thing about *you*."

Chapters 19 – 24 Match the characters in the story with the things they did.

a Antonio

b Gloria

c Tala

d Mrs. Campbell

e Riza

f Mrs. Greenstein

i received a lot of support from many different people.

ii walked Antonio up the aisle at his wedding.

iii called Tala's friends and family to tell them about the accident.

iv went into Riverview General Hospital for a hip replacement.

v remembered meeting Gloria when she was a little girl.

vi refused to allow Tala to do any housework.

B Working with Language

I Fill in the gaps with an auxiliary or a modal auxiliary verb.

a Antonio _____ worked at a different hospital before joining the staff at Riverview.

b Castillo is a fairly common name. Besides, Mr. Rosen _____ have gotten his name wrong.

....

c Daniel wasn't earning much money, so he
_____n't afford to pay for lunch.

d Gloria _____ distracted by the couple sitting
next the her on the bus.

e "_____ she met anyone at that hospital yet?"
asked Mrs. Campbell.

f If they had worked at different hospitals, Gloria and
Antonio may never _____ met each other.

2 Circle the correct word so that the sentences make sense.

a A *dinner / blind date* is when two single people who don't
know each other meet, to find out if they like each other
romantically. It's often organized by friends of the two
single people.

b Tala makes delicious *stir-fry / chargrilled* meals with chicken,
noodles and vegetables in her wok.

c If you have a fiancée or a fiancé, you are *married / engaged*.

d If a decision is unanimous, *nobody / everybody* agrees with
the decision.

e A car *ran / drove* Tala over while she was on her way to
work.

f A *wound / pulse* is an injury in which the skin has been cut
or broken.

C Activities

1 Tala believes that it is better for both halves of a couple to
come from the same culture. Do you agree? Write a blog
post presenting two arguments for Tala's view and two
against.

2 Do you think that it is a good idea for parents to try to find
partners for their children? Why / Why not?

GLOSSARY OF MEDICAL TERMS

abrasions *(n)* injuries to the skin caused by scraping

ambulance *(n)* a special vehicle used to transport ill or injured people to hospital in emergencies

antibiotics *(n)* medicine used to treat infections

bedside manner *(n)* the way a doctor or nurse talks to their patients

blood sample *(n)* blood taken from a patient to be tested to find out what is wrong with them

board-certified *(adj)* when the medical board has said that a doctor is officially qualified

cardiac arrest *(n)* when the heart stops

cardiopulmonary resuscitation (CPR) *(n)* the method used to restart a heart that has stopped

cast *(n)* a bandage stiffened and molded to the shape of a broken limb, to protect and support it while it heals

certified nursing assistant (CAN) *(n)* provides health care for people in their day-to-day living, e.g. the elderly or disabled

charts *(n)* sheets of information about a patient's medical history

complications *(n)* new problems arising from an illness or injury someone already has

coronary artery bypass *(n)* a type of heart surgery

critical *(adj)* extremely serious

diagnostic tests *(n)* tests done by a doctor or nurse to find out what is wrong with a patient

disability *(n)* a condition or injury that means you can't use a part of your body, or your brain, completely or easily

discharged *(vb)* allowed to leave the hospital

dressings *(n)* pieces of material used to cover wounds

emergency *(n)* a serious situation which requires immediate action

fatal *(adj)* causing death

femur, patella, tibia, fibula *(n)* bones in the leg

fever *(n)* an abnormally high body temperature

follow-up appointment *(n)* a patient's appointment with the doctor after leaving the hospital, to check on their progress

fractures *(n)* breaks in the bone

internal organs *(n)* important organs in the body, e.g. heart, lungs

IV *(n)* abbreviation of 'intravenous', which means medication put directly into the veins of a patient through a tube

lacerations *(n)* deep cuts or tears in the skin

licensed practical nurse (LPN) *(n)* provides basic nursing care under the direction of RNs

medications *(n)* drugs used to treat or prevent disease

nausea *(n)* feeling sick, as if you might vomit

neurological *(adj)* relating to the brain

neurosurgeon *(n)* a surgeon who specializes in operations on the brain

next of kin *(n)* your closest living relative; the person the hospital calls for you if you are injured or sick

orthopedic *(adj)* relating to bones

paramedic *(n)* a person who is trained in emergency first aid

patient *(n)* a person who has been admitted to hospital

physical therapy *(n)* the treatment of an injury by e.g. massage or exercise after, or instead of, surgery

post-operative diet *(n)* certain foods a patient must stick to after they have surgery

procedure *(n)* a surgical operation

pulse *(n)* the throbbing, felt through the skin, of blood moving through the arteries

radiologist *(n)* person who takes X-rays

recovery *(n)* the time after an illness or accident in which the patient is getting better

registered nurse (RN) *(n)* a fully trained nurse with a certificate of competence from the state

rehabilitation *(n)* the period of recovery after an illness or injury

scrubs *(n)* special hygienic clothing worn by doctors and nurses

sterile *(adj)* completely clean and free from bacteria

stethoscope *(n)* an instrument used to listen to the heartbeat

surgery *(n)* when a doctor cuts into the body to treat an illness or injury

unconscious *(adj)* not awake or aware of what's going on around you

wheelchair *(n)* a special chair with wheels used by people who cannot walk, either temporarily or permanently

wound *(n)* when the skin is cut or broken

x-rays *(n)* special photographs taken of the body to see if any bones are broken

GLOSSARY

accomplish *(vb)* to successfully complete something

affectionately *(avb)* with fondness

agony *(n)* enormous physical or emotional pain

anguished *(adj)* experiencing severe emotional pain or suffering

aide *(n)* a person whose job is to help another person, e.g. with healthcare

anticipate *(vb)* to prepare for

awkward *(adj)* embarrassing; uncomfortable

blind date *(n)* a date between two people who have not seen each other before

breakup *(n)* the end of a relationship

chemistry *(n)* the connection between two people

console *(vb)* to comfort someone who is upset

construction *(n)* building or making something as your job

contagious *(adj)* likely to spread to and affect others

dedication *(n)* being committed to a task

dependable *(adj)* can be relied on

distraught *(adj)* extremely upset

dread *(vb)* to be afraid that something bad is going to happen

dutiful *(adj)* doing what is expected of you

easygoing *(adj)* relaxed; not easily stressed

ego *(n)* your sense of self-worth

eliminate *(vb)* to get rid of someone or something

engrossed *(adj)* with all of your attention focused on something

envious *(adj)* jealous

eternity *(n)* for the rest of time

(family) function *(n)* a social gathering of family members

fidelity *(n)* faithfulness to a person

fulfillment *(n)* satisfaction with your life

handsome *(adj)* good looking, usually referring to a man

hastily *(avb)* with great speed

immature *(adj)* childish, not mature

immigrate *(vb)* to move to one country from another

impulse *(n)* a sudden strong urge to do something

incompatible *(adj)* unable to be together because of e.g. too many personality differences

intrigued *(adj)* curious about, interested in

jokingly *(avb)* playfully, meant as a joke

lab *(n)* short for 'laboratory', a room or building used for scientific research

latex *(n)* a plastic-like material used for making mostly medical products

mahjong *(n)* a Chinese game involving small wooden tiles with pictures on them

maintain *(vb)* to say something strongly and continuously

mischievously *(avb)* causing trouble in a playful way

narcissist *(n)* a person who is overly interested in themself

old-fashioned *(adj)* traditional, not modern

online dating *(n)* signing up to a website to be matched up with other people

open-minded *(adj)* willing to accept different ideas

outcome *(n)* the result of something

pedestrians *(n)* people traveling by foot

perspective *(n)* a point of view

phony *(adj)* not genuine

potential *(n)* having the capacity to develop in the future

predict *(vb)* to say something that you think will happen in the future

preoccupied *(adj)* thinking about one thing so much that you don't think about anything else

prime (of life) *(n)* the time of the greatest physical condition or personal/professional success in a person's life

reception *(n)* the party that takes place after a wedding ceremony

ritual *(n)* something that is always performed in the same way, especially in a religious ceremony

rounds *(n)* When someone visits each of a number of people, usually regularly, they 'do their rounds'.

sacrifice *(n)* something of value that someone gives up for the sake of something else they consider more important

salary *(n)* the money someone is paid each year for the work they do

scorpion *(n)* a small, poisonous insect-like creature which lives in hot countries

setback *(n)* a problem in the progress of something

sincerely *(avb)* in a genuine way

social-networking *(n)* the use of websites such as Facebook and Twitter to interact with other people

solemn *(adj)* serious

soul mate *(n)* some people believe that there is only one person for each of us, this person is your soul mate

specialize *(vb)* to become an expert in a particular area

spontaneous *(adj)* doing something without thinking, on an impulse

stabilize *(vb)* to make something steady

statement *(n)* an account of an event given to the police by a witness

supervise *(vb)* to be in charge of someone in a lower position

torment *(vb)* to cause suffering

touched *(adj)* emotionally moved

translucent *(adj)* not transparent, but allows light to pass through

unanimously *(avb)* with the agreement of all people involved

unemployed *(adj)* without a job

vaguely *(avb)* in a way that is uncertain or unclear

vulnerable *(adj)* easily hurt, physically or emotionally

widow *(n)* a woman whose husband has died

womanizer *(n)* a man who has casual affairs with numerous women

A N S W E R   K E Y

A Comprehension

Chapters 1 – 6

1 Gloria didn't want to meet Antonio because he squirted her with ketchup when she was a child, and because she didn't want her mother to interfere in her personal life.

2 Gloria thought of meeting people through friends; on online dating websites; on the bus.

3 Gloria lied so that she didn't have to agree to meet Mrs. Greenstein's grandson, Larry.

4 Tala was nervous because she was afraid of offending Riza when she told her that Gloria didn't want to meet her son.

5 Antonio didn't want to meet Gloria because he didn't have time to meet new people.

6 Tala wanted Gloria to meet somebody because she didn't want Gloria to be lonely – she wanted her to have someone in her life.

Chapters 7 – 12

7 The book *Passion on the Highlands*.

8 The view that a man needs a woman to take care of him.

9 Antonio's dream of being a doctor.

10 The man's explanation about dating several women at the same time and eliminating them one by one.

11 The moment after reflecting on all of her online dating disasters.

12 The fulfillment of being a nurse and helping people.

Chapters 13 – 18

13 Gloria to Tala, about playing mahjong with her friends.

14 Gloria to Tala, about meeting men.

15 Mr. Campbell to Mrs. Campbell, about his heart pounding when he first saw her.

16 Eliza Green to the hospital operator, about locating Gloria to tell her about Tala's accident.

17 Gloria to the other nurses, about her mother's accident.

18 Antonio to Gloria, about the fact that Gloria didn't want to meet him.

Chapters 19 – 24

a v **b** iii **c** i **d** vi **e** ii **f** iv

B Working with Language

1

a had **b** could/may/might **c** could **d** was **e** has **f** have

2

a blind date **b** stir-fry **c** engaged **d** everybody **e** ran **f** wound

C Activities

Students' own answers

 **Richmond**

58 St Aldates
Oxford
OX1 1ST
United Kingdom

Publishing Director: Deborah Tricker
Editor: Hannah Champney
Assistant Editor: Stephanie Bremner

Art Editor: Lorna Heaslip
Illustrations: Robyn Neild

Recording: EFS Television Production Ltd., Motivation Sound Studios

Printed in Spain

ISBN: 978-84-668-1736-3

DL: M-8280-2013